MW00444652

Return of the Active Manager

Return of the Active Manager

How to apply behavioral finance to renew and improve investment management

C. Thomas Howard, PhD
and Jason A. Voss, CFA

Hh

HARRIMAN HOUSE LTD
18 College Street
Petersfield
Hampshire
GU31 4AD
GREAT BRITAIN
Tel: +44 (0)1730 233870
Email: enquiries@harriman-house.com
Website: www.harriman-house.com

First published in Great Britain in 2019
Copyright © C. Thomas Howard and Jason A. Voss

The right of C. Thomas Howard and Jason A. Voss to be identified as the authors has been asserted in accordance with the Copyright, Design and Patents Act 1988.

Hardback ISBN: 978-0-85719-763-4
eBook ISBN: 978-0-85719-764-1

British Library Cataloguing in Publication Data
A CIP catalogue record for this book can be obtained from the British Library.

About the Authors

C. Thomas Howard

C. Thomas Howard, PhD is CEO and Chief Investment Officer at AthenaInvest, Inc. Tom is also Professor Emeritus at the Reiman School of Finance, Daniels College of Business, University of Denver. There he taught courses and published articles for over 30 years in the areas of investment management and international finance. Tom began as a modern portfolio theory (MPT) believer and a non-believer in active equity management. Now, due to his academic research, and professional success as an active equity manager, he is a believer in both behavioral finance and active management. As his academic colleagues say, he has turned to the dark side! Tom is a frequent speaker and author for organizations such as the CFA Institute and Investment & Wealth Institute and for publications such as the *Financial Times*, Advisor Perspectives, and ThinkAdvisor. Tom earned his BS in Mechanical Engineering from the University of Idaho, a Masters in Management Science from Oregon State University, and PhD in Finance from the University of Washington.

Professor Howard's thought leadership in behavioral finance has generated significant interest across the country with record downloads of his 'Behavioral Portfolio Management' white paper and presentations at the Investment Management Consultants Association® (now Investments and Wealth Institute) 2013 Annual Conference and CFA Institute 2014 and 2017 Annual Conferences. Articles by Dr. Howard have been among the most widely read on sites such as AdvisorPerspectives.com, CFAInstitute.org and FAmag.com.

Jason A. Voss

Jason A. Voss, CFA, is the CEO of Active Investment Management (AIM) Consulting, a firm dedicated to helping small- and medium-sized active investment managers to deliver alpha for the benefit of their end clients. He is the retired co-portfolio manager of the Davis Appreciation and Income Fund. During his tenure the Fund bested the S&P 500 by 49.1%, was Lipper #1, a Morningstar Analyst Pick, and one of the first ten funds awarded Morningstar's Stewardship Grade A. Jason also served as the Director of Content for CFA Institute, the world's largest organization of financial professionals. He is a frequent go-to interviewee for the likes of the *Wall Street Journal, Barron's*, Marketplace Morning Report, the BBC's *Today Programme*, and many others. Jason earned his BA in Economics and MBA from the University of Colorado at Boulder.

Contents

Every owner of a physical copy of this edition of

Return of the Active Manager

can download the eBook for free direct from us at Harriman House,
in a format that can be read on any eReader, tablet or smartphone.

Simply head to:

ebooks.harriman-house.com/returnactivemanager

to get your free eBook now.

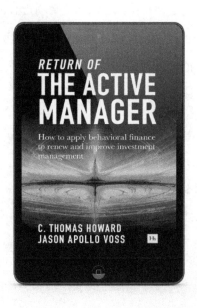

Preface

TOM AND JASON want to tell you just how excited they are that you have picked up *Return of the Active Manager* (*ROAM*). This book is about people. Specifically, our remarkable capacity to change, evolve, and get better. To blow past the status quo, ignore the naysayers, and be bigger and better than we were before.

But, in what context, you may ask? Active investing is the space in which Tom and Jason hope that you are captivated and strive to improve. Our space is all about sacrifice now for a better future. It is at its core an anticipation of something bigger and brighter if only we can forestall the urge to be and do the normal.

Tom and Jason are active investment managers. There, we said it. And at a time in which such a statement is out of favour; perhaps even old-fashioned. But to be an active manager is to believe in the largeness of human capability. To put our mind's sharp edge into the future and to slice out something remarkable. It could be something mundane, it could be something extraordinary. But the capaciousness of our minds to anticipate, to adapt, to understand, and to decide is beyond parallel. Our only obstacle is the quality of our minds, our thinking, and our behaviors. If only we can overcome the frailties of human ego, human bias, and poor judgment.

But wait! We can. We do. And we shall.

What this book is about

Return of the Active Manager provides everything for the end-client focused investment professional to begin to overcome behavioral biases, and to take advantage of them too.

You will find critical tools, including how to:

- use Big Data to reveal behavioral anomalies that are both significant and economic

- find behavioral insights in quarterly financial statements

- take advantage of in-person exchanges with the executives of businesses in which you want to invest

- the correct criteria for identifying active investment managers most likely to consistently succeed

- powerful ways of conducting in-person interviews with executive managers at businesses whose securities you analyze for possible purchase.

Who this book is for

Return of the Active Manager is for the active investment manager and those who work alongside them and around them. These people include research analysts, portfolio managers, private wealth advisors, manager search consultants, and others.

How this book is structured

We begin with a prologue which lays out the case that an entire investment ecosystem has developed unconsciously and without much evaluation. Cutting to the chase: the ecosystem is designed for passive investment products and their success. The ecosystem is one whose architecture rests on a oft-tested, consistently failed, never dismantled idea: modern portfolio theory. We request that you consider something else. Namely, behavioral finance because it is a better description of the real world and it stands up to testing.

If you accept that behavioral finance is a superior discipline then you also must demand answers, not just descriptions. It is not enough to know that human beings frequently make biased decisions. That is a given. But what do we do about that fact? How do we move beyond diagnosis to prescription? *Return of the Active Manager* moves on to describe the ways that different constituents in investment management may utilize behavioral finance to improve the lot of our end clients.

First up is a new way, a foundational way, of viewing financial markets through a behavioral lens. Following that is a heartfelt description of the most critical relationship in investing: advisors and our end clients. We put this chapter first among their prescriptions because an understanding of behavior can improve… well, everything.

Next up is Chapter 3, with insights about how investment professionals may improve their own behavior to avoid bias via bettering their processes. Fundamental analysis is frequently thought of as that most quantitative of investment activities. Yet, behavioral insights are readily available throughout this activity. Therein are critical money-making insights for investment professionals.

Our investment ecosystem has a critical gatekeeper: those conducting searches for the ace investment manager. A frequent concern among those in this community is: yes, I believe in active management, but how do I identify the good ones? Chapter 5 strives to answer these questions. Following that is a deeper dive into the ways in which pure data analysis, not only avoids much behavioral bias, but also may contribute to excellent returns.

We conclude by discussing the ways in which active investment management firms must adapt to the evolved ecosystem by changing their organizations to avoid behavioral shortcomings, and to better exalt the human analysts and decision-makers that are the beating heart of active management.

Introduction

A BURNING BRIDGE THREATENS active equity funds. Over the last ten years, large outflows have resulted in a 25% market share decline relative to passive funds, as shown in Figure A. Active US equity funds suffered $174bn outflows in 2018, equal to 4.1% of beginning assets. Meanwhile, passive US equity funds had inflows of nearly $207bn, accounting for all active US equity outflows and then some. Active US equity funds finished 2018 with 51.3% market share versus 48.7% for their passive counterparts. For perspective, the two groups started 2018 with market share of 53.9% and 46.1%, respectively. If these trends continue, passive US equity funds will surpass active funds.[1]

Investors are driving these flows as they have wised up to the value-destroying, closet-indexing gambit and are heading for the exits. There was never a question that this would eventually happen, as on average 70% of active equity funds at some point turn themselves into closet indexers and, as a result, end up delivering inferior returns to their investors. The only question was when and this has been definitively answered: right before our very eyes. Having been misled by false promises, investors are aggressively draining the closet index swamp.

---

[1]   Kevin McDevitt and Michael Schramm, '2018 U.S. Funds Flows in 5 Charts', Morningstar (2019).

The major beneficiaries of this draining have been indexing behemoths like Vanguard, BlackRock, and Schwab, who gladly scoop up the spoils of what is essentially a re-pricing of indexing services, from high-cost closet indexers to low-cost pure indexers. The highly competitive index return market is converging to a new low-cost equilibrium. And the investing public could not be happier.

The pressing question for active equity funds is, what should be done? One approach is to continue delivering beta while charging active fees and hope the fund is not caught in the ongoing swamp draining. If you pursue this route, we wish you the best of luck in surviving the scale-dominated competition, which is driving indexing fees to near zero.

Figure A: Market share of active and passive funds (2009–2018)

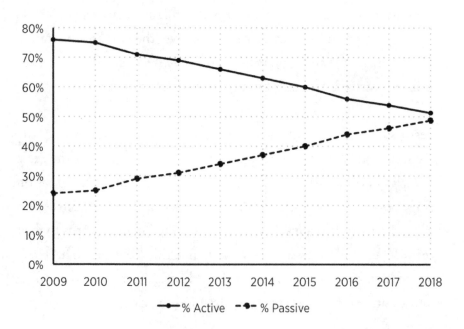

The other approach is to become truly active and deliver alpha over time, thus able to charge higher fees. This of course requires stock picking skill, which we believe is widespread within the industry, a conclusion supported by numerous studies. But in order to be truly active you will have to flaunt many an industry norm. The industry is structured to incent active funds to become closet indexers, something we refer to as the *closet indexing factory*. So, if you choose to take this less travelled alpha-generating path, you will be constantly buffeted by a hostile industry ecosystem.

In parallel to this transition, behavioral finance (BF) is becoming the paradigm of choice, replacing the discredited modern portfolio theory (MPT). While at first glance these two changes – active to passive, and MPT to BF – sweeping through the industry seem unrelated, upon closer examination they are intertwined. Unrealistic MPT concepts undergird the closet indexing factory. Full adoption of behavioral finance will lead to the dismantling of this factory, while at the same time providing a framework upon which to build an alpha-generating active equity ecosystem.

The active-passive split

An overriding question is how long will this transition from active to passive last? Will passive funds be the only ones standing at the end of the day? We do not believe this to be case for the simple reason that as uninformed passive assets under management (AUM) grows, the stock market becomes more informationally inefficient. In turn, this means information-gathering active fund performance will improve as passive AUM grows. Sanford Grossman and Joseph Stiglitz made the argument 40 years ago that some degree of information inefficiency must remain in order to incent active investors to pursue the costly process of gathering information they need to make profitable investment decisions.[2] In other words, the current passive revolution is sowing the seeds for the return of the active manager.

Russ Wermers surveyed a vast body of empirical results and concluded that the more stocks are held by passive investors, the more informationally inefficient markets become and, in turn, the greater are the opportunities for active managers.[3] In another study, Russ Wermers and Tong Yao find that passive fund trades add little to market efficiency, since they are driven by investor flows, while information-gathering active funds trade in stocks that are not efficiently priced. They find that it is often the case active and passive funds trade in the same stocks, but their trades are frequently in opposite directions.[4]

With continuing large passive inflows, stocks will be increasingly mispriced. From the 50/50 split at the time of the publication of this book, our best guess is that the forces driving flows into passive funds will eventually be neutralized by the offsetting increase in the attractiveness of stock picking, resulting in a roughly 70% passive/30% truly active split.

A 2016 study conducted by Martijn Cremers, Miguel Ferreira, Pedro Matos and Laura Starks examines the impact, across 32 countries and more than 24,000 equity funds, of what they refer to as explicit index

---

[2] Sanford Grossman and Joseph Stiglitz, 'On the Impossibility of Informationally Efficient Markets', *American Economic Review* 70 (1980), pp. 393–408.

[3] Russ Wermers, 'Active Investing and the Efficiency of Security Markets', Working Paper (2019).

[4] Russ Wermers and Tong Yao, 'Active and Passive Investing and the Efficiency of Individual Stock Prices', Working Paper (2010).

funds (as compared to closet indexers) on the performance and fees of truly active equity funds. They find that actively managed funds are more active and charge lower fees when active funds face more competitive pressure from low-cost explicitly indexed funds. Moreover, the average alpha generated by active management is higher in countries with more explicit indexing and lower in countries with more closet indexing. Overall, their evidence suggests that explicit indexing improves competition in the mutual fund industry.[5]

In other words, truly active managers should cheer the current US repricing of indexing services, from high-cost closet indexers to low-cost pure indexers. Our fondest hope is the equity investment industry will ultimately be comprised of low-cost index funds alongside truly active funds, with nary a closet indexer in sight.

We wrote this book for those equity teams who currently are or wish to become truly active and strive to generate alpha for their investors, while avoiding the temptation to turn themselves into closet indexers. We provide specific recommendations for how this can be done by means of restructuring various aspects of investment management, from client financial planning, to portfolio construction, to asset allocation, to manager selection, to security analysis, to portfolio management, to running an asset management firm.

Our goal is to help you build a viable active equity alternative so that you can successfully compete against the low-cost index funds which increasingly dominate the industry.

---

[5] Martijn Cremers, Miguel A. Ferreira, Pedro Matos and Laura Starks, 'Indexing and Active Fund Management: International Evidence', *Journal of Financial Economics* 120:3 (2016), pp. 539–560.

Prologue.
How Did We Get Here?

"The crazy thing is thinking humans act logically all the time."[6]

— Dr. Richard Thaler,
2017 Nobel Laureate in Economics,
Principal, Fuller & Thaler Asset Management

Seeing markets as they are rather than as others wish them to be

INVESTORS ARE NOT rational, and markets are not informationally efficient.

We take this as read. We no longer need to rack our brains trying to explain the illogical decisions made by investors nor crazy stock price swings. It is now widely accepted that these both are driven by investor emotions, which generate the cognitive errors of individuals and markets alike.

We both spent our early careers in the thrall of the efficient market hypothesis (EMH). Almost daily something would arise that was inconsistent with this market rationality model. But even worse, carefully researched empirical evidence piled up against the EMH.

---

[6]   *The Big Short*, Paramount Pictures (2015).

Finally, enough was enough. We abandoned both MPT and the EMH and we now fully embrace behavioral finance. We devote the time we once spent trying to explain the unexplainable to developing behaviorally-based investment management tools. This is the freedom of viewing markets as they are rather than as others wish them to be.

An interesting thing happened along the way. We discovered that viewing markets through the lens of behavior provides a superior framework for making investment decisions. This is because individuals rarely change their behavior and emotional crowds are even less likely to change theirs. On the other hand, the unrealistic rationality assumptions underlying MPT-based models produce an inferior decision framework.

Many will find this perplexing, since MPT was supposed to introduce *science* into investing via mathematical modelling. But the rationality assumptions needed to shoehorn markets into a form that could be modelled mathematically were just too extreme. The result is a theory with little or no empirical support. It turns out accepting markets as they are, full of humans with considerable emotional baggage, is superior to the neat packing provided by MPT.

We believe it is high time MPT be replaced by the far superior insights of behavioral finance. Yet, while many have written about these insights, we believe that **behavioral finance is largely a diagnosis without a prescription.**

We remedy this in this book. We take as a given that investment decision-making and the financial markets that arise from these decisions are irrational, driven by a whole swathe of behavioral biases. In our minds there is much opportunity for active investment managers to harness the resulting behavioral price distortions. In short, we seek to deliver practical applications (i.e., prescriptions) to take advantage of the insights of behavioral finance.

Much as the Renaissance of the Middle Ages transformed our world by means of careful empirical investigation rather than relying on myth and superstition, *Return of the Active Manager*, based on the empirically verified concepts of behavioral finance, will transform how we manage equity portfolios.

Evolution of the active equity ecosystem

Escaping the notice of most participants was the co-evolution of the *asset management industry* and *asset gathering industry*. The sad result is the emergence of an investment ecosystem unworkable for most truly active managers. One where they trade investment strategy freedom (long-term viability), for assets under management scale (short-term profitability). Crucially, no one party is to blame for this state of affairs. The evolution took place in the organic, diffuse way all markets evolve. Here is the evolution timeline.

1738: The rationality model

Daniel Bernoulli first proposed that individuals make rational decisions by means of maximizing expected utility.[7] This idea became the foundation for the rationality model that pervades all of the social sciences, in particular economics and later finance. MPT is an extension of the rationality model.

---

7   Daniel Bernoulli, 'Exposition of a New Theory on Measurement of Risk' (English translation of his 1738 paper in Latin), *Econometrica* 22:1 (1954), pp. 23–36.

1950s onwards: Physics envy

Physics is based on a set of mathematical laws that do a great job of describing a wide range of physical phenomena. As a result, they are the envy of the physical and social sciences. Economics began to introduce mathematical modelling in the 1950s to increase its stature within the social sciences. In the 1970s, finance bought into MPT, before it was empirically verified, in order to increase its prestige within the business school. To this day, we are paying the price for this impulsive acceptance of an unvetted MPT.

1952: MPT Pillar One: Mean-variance portfolio optimization

In 1952, Harry Markowitz proposed that investment portfolios be constructed to maximize returns for a given unit of risk via mean-variance optimization, better known as the efficient frontier.[8] His formulation was based on statistical measures and was used to demonstrate the benefits of asset allocation. Markowitz was the first to propose return variance as a measure of investment risk. His model lay dormant for a decade before being widely adopted by academics and professional investors alike.[9]

Mid-1960s: MPT Pillar Two: Capital asset pricing model

In the mid-60s, William Sharpe, John Lintner, and Jan Mossin each separately proposed what would become known as the capital asset

---

[8]   Harry Markowitz, 'Portfolio Selection', *Journal of Finance* 7:1 (1952), pp. 77–91.

[9]   Markowitz is often referred to as the father of MPT, but he recalls that Barr Rosenburg was the first to tag it with the name MPT. See Jane Wollman Rusoff's interview with Harry Markowitz, in the 15 April 2019 issue of *ThinkAdvisor*.

pricing model (CAPM). Imposing unrealistic behavioral assumptions, they were able to derive an equilibrium pricing model starting with Markowitz's mean-variance optimization. This elegant model yielded beta as the only risk measure needed for making investment decisions and a risk-adjusted combination of the market portfolio and risk-free asset as the only portfolio one need consider. A stunning simplification of truly complex investment management![10]

1967: MPT Pillar Three: Efficient market hypothesis

In what is probably the most famous finance dissertation of our generation, Eugene Fama took the rationality model to its logical conclusion that highly competitive markets will at all times drive security prices to equal underlying value.[11] Dubbed the efficient market hypothesis (EMH), it predicts that prices reflect all relevant information and thus it is not possible to earn excess returns via investment analysis. In one fell swoop, Fama declared virtually the entire investment management industry superfluous, save for index funds. Another stunning simplification of a very complex process.

---

[10]   William Sharpe, 'Capital Asset Prices – A Theory of Market Equilibrium Under Conditions of Risk', *Journal of Finance* XIX:3 (1964), pp. 425–42. Also credited with introducing the CAPM are Jan Mossin, 'Equilibrium in a Capital Asset Market', *Econometrica* 34:4 (1966), pp. 768–783; and John Lintner, 'The Valuation of Risk Assets and the Selection of Risky Investments in Stock Portfolios and Capital Budgets', *The Review of Economics and Statistics* 47:1 (1965), pp. 13–37.
[11]   Eugene Fama, 'Efficient Capital Markets: A Review of Theory and Empirical Work', *Journal of Finance* 25:2 (1970), pp. 383–417.

1970s onwards: The MPT empirical wasteland

MPT Pillar One: Mean-variance Optimization

Robert Shiller fired the first shot across the efficient frontier when in 1981 he showed that little of return volatility could be explained by changes in fundamentals, even when annual returns were examined.[12] Shiller's claim has withstood numerous challenges over the years and earned him the Nobel Prize in Economics in 2013. This means that variance and standard deviation are measuring emotionally-driven changes and not fundamental changes. So, mean-variance optimization for building long-horizon portfolios is based on a return-emotion trade-off rather than a risk-return trade-off, as initially claimed by Markowitz.

MPT Pillar Two: Capital asset pricing model

The total failure of CAPM was acknowledged by Eugene Fama and Kenneth French, who had anointed the CAPM a "theoretical tour-de-force", in 2004 when they concluded:[13]

> "The version of the CAPM developed by Sharpe (1964) and Lintner (1965) has *never* been an empirical success [emphasis ours]."

Enough said.

---

[12] Robert Shiller, 'Do stock prices move too much to be justified by subsequent changes in dividends?', *American Economic Review* 71 (1981), pp. 421–436.
[13] Eugene F. Fama and Kenneth R. French, 'The Capital Asset Pricing Model: Theory and Evidence', *Journal of Economic Perspectives* 18:3 (2004), pp. 25–46.

MPT Pillar Three: Efficient market hypothesis

The first EMH challenge came from Sanjay Basu in 1977 when he reported that stocks with low valuations, as measured by their widely publicly disseminated price-earnings ratios, consistently outperformed those with higher price-earnings ratios, dubbed the value effect.[14] The next was the 1981 Rolf W. Banz study that found small market capitalization stocks consistently outperformed large capitalization stocks even when their volatility is accounted for statistically. This is known as the 'size effect'.[15] Since then, over 300 academically-confirmed, statistically-significant *anomalies* have been uncovered.[16] The evidence against the EMH is overwhelming.

Three strikes, and MPT is out.

1984: The birth of Morningstar

Chicago in 1984 saw the birth of Morningstar, an organization that sought to evaluate mutual funds for the benefit of the general public, as well as institutional asset owners whose monies were subject to being managed by portfolio managers.

---

[14] Sanjay Basu, 'Investment Performance of Common Stocks in Relation to their Price-to-Earnings Ratios: a Test of the Efficient Market Hypothesis', *The Journal of Finance* 32:3 (1977), pp. 663–682.

[15] Banz, Rolf, 'The Relationship Between Return and Market Value of Common Stocks', *Journal of Financial Economics* 9, pp. 3–18.

[16] Campbell R. Harvey, Yan Liu, and Heqing Zhu, '… and the Cross-Section of Expected Returns', *The Review of Financial Studies* 29:1 (2016), pp. 5–68.

1992: Birth of Morningstar's style box

In response to its customers' interest in categorizing investment managers, Morningstar created the style box. The underlying assumption is that the investment strategy pursued in order to earn alpha can be fully described by the value effect and the size effect.

1992: The factor model

Faced with mounting contrary evidence, Eugene Fama and his sidekick Kenneth French launched a Hail Mary pass to salvage the efficient market hypothesis, as well as the CAPM. Both concepts were essentially dead on arrival in the 1970s and early 1980s. But Fama and French proposed a three-factor return model which included the market return, value effect, and size effect.[17] Their audacity was stunning, but the ruse worked. Rather than reject EMH as a poor description of financial markets, academics and professionals bought into the factor model hook, line, and sinker. It is now widely used for empirical tests and evaluating manager performance. Never mind that we have no idea what beta estimated based on the market return, value, and size are capturing: risk or opportunity? Fama and French are silent on this question. We are saddled with this model and we have no idea what it is telling us about markets and investment performance.

1990s to now: Convergence and synthesis

The value, size style box was a gigantic success and evolved from being a source of evaluation *after-the-fact*, to be a granite-chiselled definition of the entirety of the investment management landscape. Along with the

---

[17] Eugene Fama and Kenneth French, 'The Cross-Section of Expected Stock Returns', *The Journal of Finance* 47:2 (1992), pp. 427–465.

style box came the rise of an entirely separate industry of intermediaries whose job was to use MPT tools such as volatility, Sharpe ratios, Treynor ratios, style drift, tracking error, and many other measures, to evaluate the performance of investment managers on behalf of clients looking to allocate assets under management to investment firms. The unintentional outcome: the bland sameness in investment management strategies, leading to consistent underperformance of closet indexers, since style boxes have little to do with the investment strategy used by managers in pursuit of alpha.

MPT and style box collateral damage

As we have declared, the many concepts created in support of MPT and the style box have led to much collateral damage for active investment managers. Primarily:

- Style box based benchmarks changed from being measures of performance *after the fact* to investment constraints *before the fact*.

- For purposes of simplification, and a desire to create a robust, mathematical theory, the godfathers of MPT used measures of volatility – standard deviation and beta – as proxies for risk. This led to focusing on avoiding the short-term emotional triggers of volatility, drawdown, and tracking error. In turn, this hurt long-term equity fund performance.

- As MPT was tested, several persistent anomalies in the behavior of equity prices were identified – the value and size effects – that turned into the style box. When the style box was combined with asset allocation theory as well as performance measures based on volatility, style drift, and tracking error, active investment managers became

15

severely constrained in their creativity as they were shoehorned into a very limited number of categories of management *style*.

• When volatility-based performance measures are combined with time pressures, the net result of this short-termism is career risk for investment managers. As a result, most active managers prefer to hug their benchmarks as closely as possible and thus end up underperforming them.

• If we rewind just several decades, remember that investment managers were trying to deliver total returns and absolute returns consistently. We evaluated them the way most things are evaluated: if someone says they can do something, and it turns out that they can, then we affirm they can do that thing. When others agree to compete in the same space to achieve the same goal, we can then declare a contest, complete with rankings, including the winner.

When the performance of investment managers is compared to a stock index and all of *its* characteristics, not just its total return, then it is by definition impossible to beat the benchmark. Currently active investment managers are being asked, not just to beat the index, but to do so with the same securities, the same industry weightings, no tracking error, no style drift, the same volatility, with lower expenses, and so on.

Let's look at an example from another field. There is only one Usain Bolt. Yes, it is possible to beat Bolt in a 100-meter dash, the equivalent of a rules-based, defined context… a race. But is it possible for another sprinter to beat Bolt if he is asked to be the same height, weight, have the same stride, the same acceleration, the same lean, and so on? No. The reason is that Usain Bolt is not the standard. The standard is winning the race! This is the track and field equivalent of total return for an investment manager.

Behavioral finance to the rescue

"In physics you're playing against God, and He doesn't change His rules very often... In finance, you are playing against God's creatures, agents who value assets based on their ephemeral opinions... As a result, physicists turned quants don't expect too much from their theories, though many economists naively do."[18]

— Emanuel Derman, PhD,
Director, Program in Financial Engineering, Columbia University

Hopefully we have convinced you that MPT is not only a scientifically unverified theory, but also that it created an untenable ecosystem in which active investment managers compete. There are many responses to this, but one is: abandon MPT and its flawed ecosystem. Another response is to search for a better explanation for how markets behave. Perhaps in that explanation we can find a way to again deliver alpha for end clients. This is, of course, behavioral finance.

If you are new to behavioral finance, and many of us still are, it pays to have a basic understanding of the major biases identified through many decades of research.[19] An understanding of them is the first

---

[18] Emanuel Derman, *My Life as a Quant, Reflections on Physics and Finance* (John Wiley & Sons, 2004).

[19] Buster Benson provides a comprehensive organization of the nearly 200 cognitive biases that have been identified over the last 40 years by behavioral scientists. His work has been turned into a useful graphic, titled the Cognitive Bias Codex. See: betterhumans.coach.me/cognitive-bias-cheat-sheet-55a472476b18

step in learning to recognize them in operation within ourselves, and ultimately also benefiting from them in active investment management decision-making.

In behavioral finance we accept that financial markets are human institutions, subject to all the foibles of emotional decision making. So, at a fundamental level, consumer product markets and financial markets are little different. What is being bought and sold may differ, but how individuals go about making decisions in each type of market is quite similar.

These concepts apply whether the focus is on individuals making decisions regarding their own personal financial situation or deciding on the asset allocation within an investment portfolio, to evaluating investment managers, to making individual security buy and sell decisions. Emotions and the resulting behavior permeate every aspect of investment management, regardless of whether the person making the decision is untrained or is a highly qualified professional.

But can funds generate alpha?

Does any of this really matter, since we all *know* that active investment managers cannot beat their benchmarks?

There is, in fact, considerable evidence showing that equity active investment managers are superior stock pickers. If funds earn roughly the benchmark return after fees, which is the result found by many researchers, then before fees they must earn enough to cover fees. Indeed, Russ Wermers finds that the average stock held by equity investment managers earns a 130-basis point alpha, roughly equal to average fund fees.[20]

As discussed above, there are not only hundreds of statistically and economically significant anomalies, but there is also considerable evidence that mutual funds are able to exploit these mispricings and, in turn, deliver alpha to their investors. Jonathan Berk and Richard Green estimate that 80% of equity mutual fund managers display enough stock picking skill to cover fees, if their AUM does not grow too large.[21]

More recently, in an exhaustive meta-analysis, Martijn Cremers, Jon Fulkerson, and Timothy Riley surveyed hundreds of mutual fund studies published over the last 20 years and found many provide evidence of skilled fund managers.[22] A part of their work is pointing out potentially fatal flaws in much of the research that finds active investment management wanting. Their work sought signal among the noise and they concluded:

---

[20] Russ Wermers, 'Mutual Fund Performance: An Empirical Decomposition into Stock-Picking Talent, Style, Transactions Costs, and Expenses', *Journal of Finance* 55:4 (2000), pp. 1655–1695.

[21] Jonathan B. Berk and Richard C. Green, 'Mutual Fund Flows and Performance in Rational Markets', *Journal of Political Economy* 112:6 (2004), pp. 1269–1295. They argue that a fund manager captures the economic rents from their skill by growing the fund, since fees are generally based on the size of the fund and not on its performance. However, as the fund grows large, it becomes increasingly difficult to generate superior returns. Evidence points to $1bn as the upper AUM bound for successful stock picking.

[22] K. J. Martijn Cremers, Jon A. Fulkerson, and Timothy B. Riley, 'Challenging the Conventional Wisdom on Active Management: A Review of the Past 20 Years of Academic Literature on Actively Managed Mutual Funds', Working Paper (2018).

While the debate between active and passive is not settled and many research challenges remain, we conclude that the current academic literature finds active management more promising for investors than the conventional wisdom claims.

There is a silver lining in the rush to passive and out of active, as discussed in the Introduction. As stocks are increasingly held by index funds, which simply respond to investor flows rather than fundamental company information, stocks become increasingly mispriced. This phenomenon is confirmed by Russ Wermers and Tong Yao who found that stocks with 'excessive' levels of passive fund ownership and trading exhibit more long-term pricing anomalies as well as a larger price reversal following trades.[23]

The implication is that as investors flee closet indexers and move their money into low-cost index funds, stock picking opportunities improve. This is good news for those who want to run truly active equity funds.

We now turn to the prescriptions for successful active equity management. In Chapter 1 we lay out the behavioral foundation upon which remaining chapters rest.

---

[23] Russ Wermers and Tong Yao, 'Active vs. Passive Investing and the Efficiency of Individual Stock Prices', University of Maryland Working Paper (2010).

Chapter 1.
Behavioral Financial Markets

At a crossroads

B RUCE BENNETT WAS at a crossroads. He was well on his way to becoming a respected investment consultant, a profession in which it was thought difficult for investment managers to consistently beat their benchmarks. But he kept coming across investing strategies that were beating benchmarks, and by wide margins. This was unsettling as these superior returns were not being arbitraged away over time. He thought, 'How could this be in light of the widely-held belief of informationally-efficient markets?'

Most recent was Bruce's discovery of a strategy named Profiting from Media Outrage created by Dr. Richard Peterson, who developed Thomson Reuters' MarketPsych Indices.[24] Peterson and his team's simple strategy held the 20 stocks most scorned by social media and the press. Each stock was chosen using objective criteria, held for a year, and featured monthly trading. In defiance of the efficient market hypothesis, the strategy beat the S&P 500 in all but two years from 1999 through early 2018, besting the broad market by an average of over 10% annually. Bruce found himself again asking, 'How could this be?'

---

[24]   Richard Peterson at www.marketpsych.com.

Straightforward yet emotionally difficult

Bruce observed that many of the most successful strategies, including Peterson's, were straightforward, yet crucially they were also *emotionally difficult* to implement. He concluded such strategies were likely to continue working because they were based on the collective emotions of investors, and he was aware that people rarely alter their behavior. Another crucial factor to successful implementation required decision-making immune to the very emotional behaviors creating the alpha opportunities in the first place. In other words, implementation was emotionally challenging for the manager.

As Bruce thought about how to encourage pursuit of successful strategies for the benefit of the investing public, it slowly dawned on him that the techniques he and his fellow investment consultants used to select and evaluate managers discouraged investment teams from pursuing profitable strategies.

It turns out asking managers to minimize style drift, tracking error, volatility, and drawdown encouraged investment teams to react in lockstep with the emotional crowds, thus negating the possibility for outperformance. Bruce recognized that each of these represent an emotional trigger for investors and by minimizing them, the fund was catering to investor emotions. The problem is that each is also characteristic of successful active management, as it is necessary to differ from the benchmark in order to beat the benchmark. Minimizing these portfolio characteristics is the path to closet indexing.

Bruce thought to himself, 'Don't I want to encourage rather than discourage superior performance?' Before addressing this question, he needed a new conceptual market framework on which he could build a new approach. Bruce was convinced that he must first accept markets as they are – irrational, and thus full of opportunities – rather than how many in the industry thought they should be – rational, and thus devoid of opportunity. But what was this better way of viewing markets?

Seeing markets as they are

"Indeed, we have to distance ourselves from the presumption that financial markets always work well and that price changes always reflect genuine information… The challenge for economists is to make this reality a better part of their models."

— Robert Shiller in 'From Efficient Markets Theory to Behavioral Finance'[25]

Professor Shiller wrote these words in 2003. Ten years later he received the 2013 Nobel Prize in Economics for his pioneering behavioral finance research, sharing the prize with Lars Peter Hansen and Eugene Fama. Naming Professor Fama as co-recipient created a Machiavellian buzz in anticipation of the award ceremony, as Shiller had described Fama's efficient market hypothesis as "the most remarkable error in the history of economic thought." Who says the Nobel committee doesn't have a twisted sense of humor?

Behavioral finance received a further boost in 2017 when the Nobel Prize in Economics was awarded to Richard Thaler of the University of Chicago, also home to Fama. Thaler throughout his career has focused on the cognitive errors made by individuals and how government

---

[25] Robert Shiller, 'From Efficient Markets Theory to Behavioral Finance', *Journal of Economic Perspectives* 17:1 (2003), pp. 83–104.

and business policy can be revised to *nudge* people to make better decisions.[26]

Today, behavioral finance appears everywhere in the financial services industry. Advisors are warming to the notion that behavioral coaching is important for the successful execution of a client's financial plan. Many are concluding that such coaching should represent a significant portion of time spent with clients. And, in fact, many products are springing up to help advisors support their clients' pursuit of rational outcomes in the face of many possible emotional stressors.

Since Shiller's statement over 15 years ago, an avalanche of new academically-verified pricing anomalies have appeared to further challenge the notion "that price changes always reflect genuine information." This has now gotten to the point that we must wonder if collective cognitive errors are the primary drivers of investment returns, displacing new information as the most important driver.

Understanding investor behavior is the best way to understand markets

Viewing investors and markets as emotional decision-makers rather than as rational computational entities forces us to reconsider every aspect of how we operate in financial markets. Shifting to a behavioral perspective is a critical first step. After recognition comes a formal transition to improved analytic tools.

---

[26]   Richard Thaler, *Misbehaving: The Making of Behavioral Economics* (W. W. Norton & Company, 2015).

As Shiller suggests, it is time to move away from the efficient market hypothesis, one of the pillars of modern portfolio theory, to a more promising alternative: behavioral financial markets.[27] The four behavioral financial market concepts we discuss below provide a framework for rethinking client financial planning, asset allocation, investment manager selection and evaluation, and the creation and execution of investment strategies, each of which is discussed in the chapters that follow.

Four foundational concepts

There are four concepts we believe underpin behavioral financial markets (BFM):[28]

1. Market prices are mainly driven by emotional crowds.

2. Investors are not rational, financial markets are not informationally efficient.

3. There are hundreds of behavioral price distortions (anomalies) that investors can exploit.

4. Managing emotions is the most important determinant of long-horizon wealth.

---

[27] Robert Shiller, *Irrational Exuberance* (Princeton University Press, Third Edition, 2015).

[28] Two recent alternative models view the market as an ecosystem best understood using biological and evolutionary concepts rather than physics like laws: Andrew W. Lo, *Adaptive Markets: Financial Evolution at the Speed of Thought* (Princeton University Press, 2017); and the notion of investor-driven stock characteristic popularity, Roger G. Ibbotson, Thomas M. Idzorek, Paul D. Kaplan, and James X. Xiong, 'Popularity: A Bridge between Classical and Behavioral Finance', CFA Institute Research Foundation (2018).

BFM Concept 1: Market prices are mainly driven by emotional crowds, not fundamentals

We have difficulty understanding why markets and their underlying securities move the way they do over shorter time periods. This is disconcerting as we are investment professionals and our clients expect us to understand and explain what at times are unsettling, if not downright terrifying, market movements. But the truth is that most individual security and market movements are inexplicable because they are driven by emotional crowds for no identifiable reason.

An entire media and professional ecosystem has grown up to fill this information void. Market events are continuously ascribed to one new piece of information or event. On every single day a reason is given by the media for why the market did what it did. This is because people understand the world by means of narratives and the more detailed the story, the more believable it becomes in the eyes of the public.

When asked about why the market went down today, Tom responds: "I have no idea why the market went down today. Some days it goes up and some days it goes down and I don't know why. But I do know 55/65/75: the stock market produces a positive return in 55% of days, 65% of months, and 75% of years. I like those odds and so I keep playing this game over and over!"

Rarely does the press ask Tom's opinion regarding daily market movements as he lacks the kind of narrative that resonates with investors. Meanwhile, Jason has stated for many years that his success has never been based on an understanding of financial markets, which he finds inexplicable in their daily gyrations.

So, if you are asked by clients why the market, a stock, or other security moved the way it did on a day, the honest answer is most often, "I have no idea." Unsettling as this may be, it is the consequence of the first BFM concept: emotions – not fundamentals – are the main movers of financial markets.

Some may feel that admitting much of what happens in markets cannot be explained means that as an investment professional we have little to offer. But quite the contrary, this admission is the first step towards providing greater client value. Financial markets cannot be easily explained or neatly packaged into a set of mathematical equations. Markets are noisy and largely unpredictable and the only way to operate successfully in them is to avoid being fooled by this messiness.

One final point before moving on. The exceptionally small percentage of the market that trades each day means that when there are, in fact, emotional stressors present in the news, it does not take too many additional trades to create wild price swings.[29] After all, securities prices are set by the small number of marginal buyers and sellers.

Do investor errors offset one another?

One possible issue to consider here, and you may have thought of it yourself while digesting this chapter, is whether different investors' irrational behaviors offset one another, and still result in an efficient pricing mechanism. Stated differently, aren't markets always about

---

[29] According to data from the World Federation of Exchanges and the World Bank, the average daily turnover for world stock markets from 1992 to 2017 was 0.29%. In other words, 0.29% of stocks are traded on each day. During periods of heightened emotion, such as the Great Recession in 2008, the global averaged bumped up to 0.34%.

bidders and askers, demanders and suppliers disagreeing with one another? Thus, while individual investors may be irrational, in the aggregate they are rational, right?

We offer up our own data in Table 1.1 that shows that the average high-low spread, relative to annual average level of stocks in the S&P 500, is 22.5% from 1950 through September 2018.

Table 1.1: Average relative annual S&P 500 high-low spread

Decade	Average S&P 500 high-low spread
1951–1960	20.7%
1961–1970	20.7%
1971–1980	23.6%
1981–1990	23.9%
1991–2000	20.7%
2001–2010	28.5%
2011–Sep 2018	17.6%
Overall average	22.5%

Source: Yahoo! Finance.

Why does this high-low spread matter?

If financial market prices are supposedly rationally determined, based on responses to new information, does it make sense that the average annual range for an entire broad index, relative to its average level in a year, is 22.5%?

After all, the actual economic value of the companies making up the S&P 500 does not fluctuate by 22.5% in a year. For example, Proctor & Gamble stably sells millions of units each year over broad and numerous product categories and has done so for decades. Therefore, it is not rational that its price would fluctuate radically out of step with its actual economic value.

At most we would expect its value to fluctuate tightly around the actual expected economic value of the business. Clearly for such large and long-lived businesses like those that compose the S&P 500, an average fluctuation of such *magnitude* defies common sense. Instead, the average fluctuation of 22.5% is evidence of the very irrationality predicted by behavioral finance. This is consistent with investor irrationality first proposed by Nobel Laureate Robert Shiller in 1981 and confirmed by numerous academic studies since then.[30]

BFM Concept 2: Investors are not rational, financial markets are not informationally efficient

The concepts of behavioral financial markets run counter to the major pillars of 20th-century financial theory: that investors are expected utility maximizers and market prices reflect all relevant information.

Behavioral science research decimates the expected utility maximizer concept. It is virtually impossible for an individual to collect all needed information and then accurately process that information to come up with a rational decision. This is known as bounded rationality, first introduced by economist Herbert Simon.[31]

---

[30]   Robert Shiller, 'Do stock prices move too much to be justified by subsequent changes in dividends?', *American Economic Review* 71 (1981), pp. 421–436.
[31]   Herbert Simon, 'Behavioral Model of Rational Choice', in *Models of Man, Social and Rational: Mathematical Essays on Rational Human Behavior in a Social Setting* (Wiley, 1957).

Even more damaging, Daniel Kahneman, Amos Tversky, and others convincingly demonstrate that even when all information is available, individuals are highly susceptible to cognitive errors. As Kahneman and Tversky concluded after years of research, human beings are by and large irrational decision-makers.[32]

Since we are strongly predisposed to make cognitive mistakes due to our emotions, then it takes only a small step to conclude that markets cannot be informationally efficient. The evidence supporting this conclusion is vast: as we stated earlier there are hundreds of statistically verified anomalies in the academic literature and more continue to be found. The result is a bleak picture: emotional investors, burdened by cognitive biases, with a penchant for herding, regularly driving prices away from underlying fundamental value.

But all is not lost

Unexpectedly, analyzing investors and markets through a behavioral lens provides a more reliable framework. Why? Because, as you know, most of us find it hard to change our behaviors. And crowds are even less inclined to alter their collective behavior.

Financial advisors are building practices around the behavioral concepts and biases uncovered over the last 40 years by behavioral scientists such as Daniel Kahneman and Amos Tversky. The resulting financial plan and ongoing coaching are anchored in behaviors that are unlikely to change any time soon (see Chapter 2).

---

[32] Daniel Kahneman, *Thinking, Fast and Slow* (Farrar, Straus and Giroux, 2011).

Portfolio managers and analysts are building strategies based on measurable and persistent behavioral factors, frequently using fundamental data as an objective proxy for these factors (see Chapter 4). The well-known result that individuals and groups are loathe to change their behavior means these funds have an excellent chance of long-term outperformance.

Consultants and investment platform analysts can focus on behavior as well (see Chapter 5). They need to create incentives to encourage high-performance behavior by investment managers. According to academic studies and industry analysis, including Tom's own research, high-performance behaviors include consistently pursing a narrowly defined strategy, while taking only high-conviction portfolio positions.[33] To date, the focus has been on reducing short-term volatility, style drift, and tracking error. Changing incentives will lead to funds behaving in a way that builds long-horizon wealth for investors.

BFM Concept 3: There are hundreds of behavioral price distortions (anomalies) that can be used for building superior portfolios

When an event like the surprise 2016 Brexit vote in the United Kingdom triggers the emotions of market participants, most react in a similar way. In the first hours following the vote, markets were sharply down. (Remember loss aversion!) This collective response is further amplified by herding. Indeed, herding can occur even without an external event.

---

[33]   See Tom's working paper 'The Importance of Investment Strategy' (March 2010) and Randy Cohen, C. Polk, and B. Silli, 'Best Ideas', Harvard Working Paper (2010).

We collectively react because we see everyone else reacting, even if we do not know the reason for the sudden stampede.

Emotional crowds rampaging in markets create numerous opportunities for professional investors who are not caught up in the moment. We refer to these opportunities as behavioral price distortions. Alternatively, these are dubbed *anomalies* in the academic literature because their existence is inconsistent with the efficient market hypothesis. When they are included in asset pricing models or in constructing smart beta portfolios, they are called *factors*. We prefer the term *behavioral price distortions* because this suggests that they are the consequence of collective emotional behavior.

A comprehensive list of academically-verified distortions can be found on Campbell Harvey's website.[34] The long-short returns for some of the best-known distortions can be found on Ken French's website and the long-term performance of a sample of these is reported in Table 1.2.[35]

Table 1.2: Behavioral price distortions (1927–2018)

Return series	Annual return
Market–Risk free	8.34%
Small–Big (Size effect)	3.12%
High Book-to-Market–Low (Value effect)	4.73%
High–Low (Momentum)	9.24%

Source: Ken French's website.

---

[34] See faculty.fuqua.duke.edu/~charvey/Factor-List.xlsx for an Excel spreadsheet of the over 300 academically-verified behavioral price distortions.
[35] See Ken French's website for monthly and daily returns for various price distortions: mba.tuck.dartmouth.edu/pages/faculty/ken.french/data_library.html

These are but a few of the attractive price distortion return opportunities available to analysts when building an investment strategy. These distortions are some of the ingredients active managers use when creating a strategy.

In the case of smart beta portfolios, they are the entire strategy. These are often referred to as *dumb alpha* since these portfolios replicate a distortion-tilted index, such as investing in low PE stocks in order to capture the value effect.

For other active managers, distortions represent only a portion of the strategy because an investment manager's *recipe* or decision-making process makes up the rest. For example, fundamental investment teams conduct primary research on the companies in which they are interested by means of financial analysis, understanding its product lines and operations, interviewing the management team, surveying the competitive environment in which the company operates, and other important aspects of the company (see Chapter 4). In this case, identified price distortions are used to augment the strategy, such as considering the PE ratio or using momentum as part of the decision to buy and sell stocks.

Behavioral price distortions are frequent contributors to successful active management.

BFM Concept 4: Dealing with emotions at each stage of the investment process is the most important determinant of long-horizon wealth

Managing client emotions

Emotions and the resulting behavior are the most important consideration in managing a client's investment portfolio. The process begins with client needs-based planning, in which a separate portfolio is built for each different need. This initial planning phase is critical to removing investor emotional errors from the wealth-building process.

For the growth portion of the portfolio, the focus is on a long investment horizon. The task of the advisor is to encourage clients to adopt a long-term view while avoiding emotional reactions to short-term events. Evidence indicates that such myopic-loss-averting decisions have a profoundly negative effect on wealth.[36] Emotional coaching is one of the most important services an advisor can offer clients (see Chapter 2).

If needs-based planning is successful, the money allocated to the growth portion of the client's portfolio can be largely invested in high-expected-return but short-term-volatile securities like equities. Admittedly, it is a challenge to keep clients fully invested while avoiding costly trading decisions when markets turn volatile.

Harnessing behavioral price distortions

Portfolio managers and their analysts must deal with emotions at several levels. When building an investment strategy, only those behavioral

---

[36] Shlomo Benartzi and Richard Thaler, 'Myopic Loss Aversion and the Equity Premium Puzzle', *Quarterly Journal of Economics* (1995).

price distortions that have been shown to be measurable and persistent based on careful and thoughtful analysis should be accepted. For example, while Fed actions and interest rates are often put forward as reasons for market movements, there is precious little evidence of such causality.

The goal is to focus only on those distortions supported empirically by large data or real-world experience while ignoring everything else. As a result, investment teams become expert at filtering the signal from the considerable noise in the market. This means they may not be able to explain daily events, but they are able to deliver long-horizon wealth to clients.

Strategy implementation

In implementing a strategy, it is important not to succumb to the same emotions as do non-professionals. There is now considerable research showing how fund managers can avoid making the cognitive errors so detrimental to portfolio returns.[37] For example, do not fall in love with your investments, but instead remove the emotions by developing an objective selling rule.

Fund manager evaluation

For consultants and investment platform analysts, the challenge is to avoid baking investor emotions into the criteria used for selecting and evaluating managers. Individuals react strongly to short-term volatility and drawdowns as well as tracking error, even when facing a long time

---

[37]   See, for example, Claire Flynn Levy at Essentia Analytics, www.essentia-analytics.com.

horizon. These emotions are best dealt with by means of careful financial planning, multi-strategy portfolios, and advisor emotional coaching.

But many in this position respond to the lowest common denominator by expecting every fund to manage each of these emotional triggers by reducing short-term volatility and tracking error. This results in underperforming portfolios and the reduction in long-horizon wealth. There is a high price to be paid by investors when emotional catering is demanded of each and every fund, for each and every period.

Our clients can only spend absolute returns, and not emotions, or the volatility caused by them. So, the focus by advisor, fund manager, and analyst alike should always be on long-term wealth creation, which is dependent on not indulging our and their emotions.

Chapter review and what is to come

Collective, emotionally-driven behavior is the foundational concept underlying behavioral financial markets. Markets are populated by human investors burdened with emotional baggage and associated cognitive errors. These errors are amplified inside a market due to herding and thin participation, leading to wild price swings. Rampaging emotional crowds are the cause of excess return volatility. As Shiller points out in his book *Irrational Exuberance*, you need look no further than equity market price bubbles for evidence of the dramatic effect of emotional crowds.

Of course, economic, political, international and market information flows continuously into markets. In times past, it was thought that the arrival of these pieces of new information was the primary reason prices moved the way they did, as participants rationally processed and repriced securities. But this idyllic concept has now been shredded and replaced with emotional crowds as the most important drivers.

Fundamental information, rather than being front and center, works behind-the-scenes in the investment process of professional money managers. And if one takes a long enough perspective, it also influences the returns of individual securities and markets. The most economically successful companies earn the highest return over the long run and the reason the stock market goes up over time is directly related to growth in the underlying economy.

The pecking order has changed, with emotional crowds dominating prices and returns over shorter periods, with fundamentals holding sway only over longer periods. For those who spend time making investment decisions, this is not surprising. But for many in the academic and professional communities, this represents a sea change in how to think about and analyze markets. That is, when trying to understand price changes in the short term, the focus should be on emotions and resulting behavior rather than on fundamentals.

Taking liberties with Professor Shiller's quote above, "The challenge for investment professionals is to make this reality a better part of their models." In other words, see markets as they are rather than how others would like them to be. The analytical tools derived from behavioral financial markets' more realistic representation of financial markets are the focus of the remainder of this book.

Chapter 2.
Prescriptions for Financial Advisors

The return of volatility

A S FRANK CARLSON walked into his office in Denver in February 2018, he was preoccupied with the financial events of the last few weeks. After a period of market tranquillity over the previous 12 months, volatility had returned with a vengeance. The previous week had seen the largest single day jump in the history of the VIX. His clients were expressing concern about the duration of the current bull market and whether they should move to cash.

Recent history weighed on his mind as well. Since the Great Recession, investors had withdrawn hundreds of billions of dollars from US equity mutual funds. Estimated losses in the stock market alone in 2008 totalled $6.9trn and many investors stayed on the sidelines for years, missing the opportunity to recover their wealth.[38]

As volatility returned to normal and client questions abounded about the market, Frank knew he had to focus on client behavioral coaching

---

[38]   Renae Merle, 'Wall Street's Final '08 Toll: $6.9 Trillion Wiped Out', *Washington Post* (1 January 2009).

in the coming weeks, hoping to prevent panicky sell-off requests that he knew would destroy his client's long-term wealth.

A changing industry

It was Frank's belief that the massive push of low-cost index products in recent years combined with the long bull market had led many investors to view investing as a commodity. For many, investment decision-making was considered as easy as simply buying the lowest-cost investment.

To add value above and beyond the rapidly expanding robo advisor/index fund model, Frank began to provide planning and behavioral coaching as part of his service offering. In addition, he joined the emerging category of advisors who go beyond simple reactive coaching, because he believed the current situation provided a challenge as well as an opportunity to take the next step toward becoming a behavioral wealth advisor.

Frank was convinced that investor emotions and the resulting behaviorally-driven decisions were the most important determinant of long-horizon wealth. He saw behavioral coaching as a valuable part of his practice, something that a robo-advisor cannot provide. This is because it allows his clients to stay calm when markets turn choppy, as well as stay invested in actively managed funds, which he believes provide superior returns over the long term versus index funds.

With these thoughts in mind, Frank prepared for his first meeting of the day, a client who had expressed considerable anxiety about the recent return of market volatility.

Differentiation as a behavioral wealth advisor[39]

We start our story at the beginning, with financial advisors who play a critical role in helping clients avoid the emotional mistakes that are so detrimental to building long-horizon wealth. Advisors serve on the front line of the transition from MPT to behavioral finance. Examining the ongoing adoption of behavioral finance concepts within this community provides an early glimpse into the change that will eventually sweep through the consultant, investment platform analyst, and portfolio management communities that we discuss in later chapters.

A behavioral wealth advisor (BWA) takes a holistic and proactive approach to wealth management, creating a behavioral discipline throughout the client service model that is designed to increase the client's confidence and minimize behavioral biases. Based on our experience in working with hundreds of advisors, making the changes we describe later in this chapter results in better client relationships and a more successful practice.

As support for these statements, Cerulli Associates finds that advisors who focus on the client experience rather than on their own investment expertise grow faster with larger average clients who display greater loyalty.[40]

On the planning front, Annamaria Lusardi and Olivia Mitchell found that those who set up and stuck with a plan ended up with three times more wealth than those who did no planning at all, as shown in

---

[39] Material for this chapter is drawn from 'The Behavioral Wealth Advisor' published in the July/August 2018 issue of *Investments & Wealth Monitor*.
[40] www.cerulli.com

Figure 2.1.[41] The concepts of planning, being a quarterback of a stable of outside experts, and helping clients avoid emotional mistakes are central to being a BWA and, in turn, this results in a growing, successful practice.

Figure 2.1: Total net worth across different planning types

Had and Stuck to the Plan	Had a Savings Plan	Calculated Retirement Needs
		$742,843
$1,002,975	**$910,382**	No Retirement Plan
		$338,418

Source: Annamaria Lusardi and Olivia Mitchell, 'Financial Literacy and Planning: Implications for Retirement Wellbeing', NBER 2011.

As the wealth management industry evolves to accommodate changing investor demands, a host of new players are now available to service them. The robo-advisor, for example, offers financial solutions through full automation with low to no cost, putting pressure on advisors to justify their fees. By contrast, the BWA addresses the client's full suite of comprehensive financial needs and provides more custom planning and behavioral guidance.

As we discussed earlier, investors often make decisions based on their emotions rather than on logic and historical data, even with the data right in front of them.[42] Evidently the conditioning around money that we are raised with or experience as adults leads to detrimental behaviors in investment decision-making. Triggering events can produce common

---

[41] Annamaria Lusardi and Olivia Mitchell, 'Financial Literacy and Planning: Implications for Retirement Wellbeing', NBER Working Paper (2011).

[42] Daniel Kahneman, *Thinking, Fast and Slow* (Farrar, Straus and Giroux, 2011).

emotional reactions and cognitive errors. We all know these mistakes can be expensive, but investors who work with a BWA have a much better chance of avoiding them.

Indeed, research by Vanguard,[43] Russell Investments[44] and others has quantified the value of behavioral guidance in terms of investor returns, estimating that it makes up between one-third to one-half of annual returns!

This research is helping to educate advisors about their full potential value to end clients, which can be realized only when combining investment solutions, financial planning, and behavioral guidance, as illustrated in Figure 2.2.

Figure 2.2: An advisor's full potential value

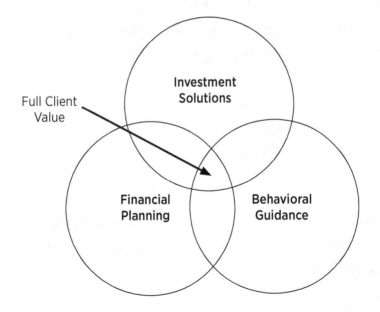

_____

[43]   Vanguard, 'Quantifying Your Value to Clients' (2016).
[44]   Russell Investments, 'Why Advisors Have Never Been So Valuable' (2017).

Key investing principles

"Our brain is old, hungry, and impatient. It has not evolved for 150,000 years, it consumes 20% of each day's energy while representing only 3% of body weight and makes decisions quickly since it is optimized for a world populated by 300-pound javelinas, 12-foot monitor lizards, and sabertooth tigers."

— Daniel Crosby in *The Behavioral Investor*[45]

With the important role of the BWA established, let's now move on to look at a set of fundamental investment principles that we consider to be pillars of a behavioral wealth advisory practice.

Reframing risk beyond volatility

One core principle is recognizing short-term volatility in the stock market for what it is, the emotions of buyers and sellers. Volatility is a natural phenomenon of a marketplace and it is the price one pays for the return premium of equities.

Volatility is not a risk for long-horizon portfolios, despite our industry's mistaken use of volatility as a risk measure (e.g., risk tolerance, drawdown, standard deviation, tracking error). A long-term equity investor can learn to expect short-term movements in the equity markets and ignore them, much as they would the turbulence on an airplane flight. Investors should focus on their ultimate destination: their goals and long-term returns.

---

[45] Daniel Crosby, *The Behavioral Investor* (Harriman House, 2018).

We consider the most common and most critical type of risk in the growth portion of a portfolio to be underperformance risk or leaving money on the table, which most often translates to the opportunity cost of not having adequate exposure to equities. Our clients cannot spend beta, or standard deviation, but they can spend money.

Looking historically, the opportunity cost of trying to avoid volatility is significant. For example, the retiree who has been overly conservative in equity holdings faces the potential of running out of money, instead of enjoying long-term equity returns.

As shown in Figure 2.3, over the 30 years ending December 31, 2017, stocks (the S&P 500) returned 10.6% versus 6.4% for bonds (10-year US Treasury notes) and 3.1% for cash (three-month US Treasury bills).

The differences in returns are significant. In dollars, the differences are even more pronounced. Over the 30 years, $10,000 in cash netted $24,728, bonds provided $65,123, and stocks earned $205,557. Avoiding stocks due to volatility means settling for much lower returns.

Active equities for wealth creation

Understanding the importance of active equity investing in the creation of long-term wealth is another pillar of behavioral wealth advising. The overwhelming presence of emotions involved in investment decisions creates recurring inefficiencies in the marketplace. Those inefficiencies, when systemically analyzed, can generate terrific opportunities for superior investment selection and portfolio performance. Consequently, we see active equity portfolios as the most effective contributors to client wealth-creation and the achievement of their financial goals.

Figure 2.3: Annual returns for 30 years through 2017

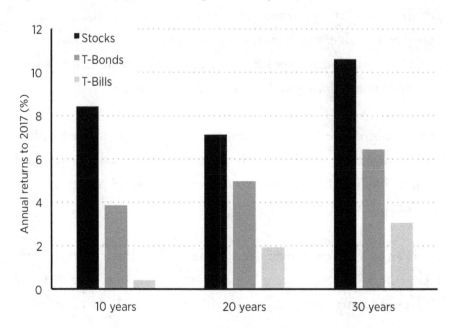

Annualized returns as of December 31, 2017: Stocks (S&P 500); Bonds (10-year US Treasury Note); Cash (three-month US Treasury Bill). Source: New York University, pages.stern.nyu.edu/~adamodar/New_Home_Page/datafile/histretSP.html.

Planning is key and investing is a long-term endeavor

Planning is the most effective way to allocate money to meet short and long-term needs. It improves long-term performance by investing money based on real client needs rather than over-indulging emotions that masquerade as legitimate concepts of risk tolerance. In addition, planning increases client confidence and comfort by making sure that both short- and long-term financial needs are met.

When planning is combined with a long-term investing approach, it almost entirely removes emotions from the equation and investors sleep better at night. Clients also are more apt to ignore media hype about daily events if they understand the reality of short-term volatility and understand that investing is a long-term endeavor. Planning helps them to accept that short-term volatility is the expression of many people's deeply felt anxieties and biases, rather than a sophisticated judgment of investment opportunities by the cognoscenti.

Although we know from extensive research that we cannot accurately forecast annual market returns, we do know from long-term market history the rule of 55/65/75: The stock market produces a positive return in 55% of days, 65% of months, and 75% of years. The BWA helps their clients to understand this, to encourage them to take a long-term view.

BWA client service model

A BWA manages a client's overall financial plan, including services performed by external parties. As such, the suggestions provided here apply to services that the advisor directly manages, as well as services integrated into the financial plan, such as risk management, tax planning, and estate planning.

The BWA's ideal client is one who is confident that all aspects of the financial plan are appropriately considered and managed in an integrated fashion. As illustrated in Figure 2.4, the BWA is the client's central point of contact for any questions or issues that arise.

Figure 2.4: Relationship model – matching needs and solutions

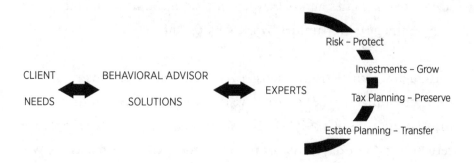

Every step of the BWA client service model address and mitigates behavioral biases. We view the client service model in two distinct sections, the front-end process and ongoing servicing. Figure 2.5 illustrates the overall process and each component is described in more detail below.

Figure 2.5: Service process model

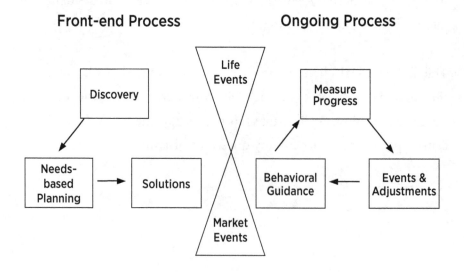

Step 1: Discovery

The main goal of discovery is to gather the financial and emotional data needed to create a financial plan and to determine the best approach to working with the client based on the client's behavioral profile. This is the opportunity to understand the client's goals, behaviors, and perceptions about risk. It means asking thoughtful questions about the client's values and motivations, and understanding how the client made prior investment decisions.

An important take-away should be a behavioral profile for each client. By segmenting clients into persona types, you can tailor the communications process and plan more appropriately for meetings.

Figure 2.6, for example, shows Morningstar's behavioral profiles, which are segmented by time horizon and control.[46]

The BWA also should assess if the firm's capabilities align well with the client's needs and desires. If the client appears to be a good fit, the final discovery step is to get a complete financial picture so that the advisor and client have a comprehensive understanding of resources available and of what is already in place. This includes financial assets and liabilities, income and expenses, insurance, wills, trusts, and other important relationships such as spouses, dependents, trustees, and beneficiaries.

---

[46]   Morningstar, 'Simple But Not Easy' (2017).

Figure 2.6: Behavioral profiles example

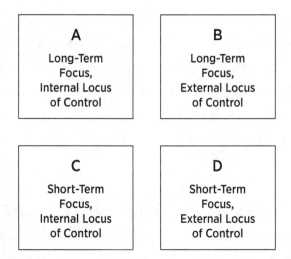

Step 2: Needs-based planning

Once the advisor-client relationship has been formally established and the client's current financial situation has been fully inventoried, it's time to move to planning.

The plan can help manage client behaviors over time if it is carefully designed to meet their needs, separating them according to short term and long term. This separation feature allows for a portfolio of liquid assets to meet emergency needs and income, if necessary, over a three-to five-year period, so there is no need to liquidate the stock portion of the portfolio. Separating assets dedicated to growth is also important to reduce concerns about the future. The plan is managed continually to keep short-term needs in balance with long-term growth.

Needs-based planning goes a long way in reducing client anxiety and building client feelings of confidence, control, and comfort because the client is continually reassured that their full set of financial needs are being met. The BWA designs a plan to address the client's principal needs, as illustrated in Figure 2.7. The plan has a disciplined process for coordinating with experts about more specialized needs. This includes protecting the client from the potentially devastating impact of various unexpected life events that may otherwise endanger the plan (risk management), optimizing the plan for net income (tax management), and customizing the plan with the intelligent divestiture of wealth according to the client's wishes (estate planning).

Figure 2.7: Needs-based planning

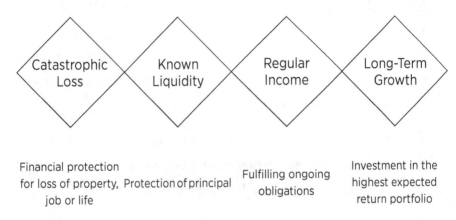

The advisor's client-management goal at this step is to ensure that the client is confident in the plan details. This confidence will help maintain the discipline to follow the plan during difficult life stages and market events. The most critical step in establishing this confidence is to comprehensively identify needs within the following five distinct financial areas:

1. *Catastrophic risks.* Clients need to insure against the large financial risks associated with unpredictable catastrophic life events. Although insurance and investing are distinct areas of expertise, no financial

plan is complete without a thoughtful plan for high-impact risks such as death of a spouse, long-term disability, and liability exposure.

2. *Known liquidity.* This category includes known future expenses beyond normal household operating expenses that are expected in the next three to five years. Job transitions, new vehicles, or planned vacations can be among these expenses. From a behavioral perspective, the idea is to provide a very high level of confidence that the client's short-term liquidity needs are completely covered.

3. *Regular income.* For clients still in the workforce, this need usually is met with household earnings from employment. For those in retirement, the need is calculated as the shortfall of combined monthly income from Social Security and pension payments versus monthly expenses. Any ongoing distributions for the next three to five years should be considered.

4. *Long-term capital growth.* All assets not committed to short-term liquidity or income generation should be dedicated to investments focused on growth and long-horizon wealth accumulation.

5. *Estate and legacy.* For those clients who have successfully covered the first four needs, the focus shifts to financial stewardship and how a lifetime of accumulated wealth can be best utilized in the future. These needs can include the financial well-being of children and grandchildren, or contributing toward a cherished cause.

Step 3: Solutions

Now that all the client's needs have been captured in the planning process, the advisor can seek the optimal solution to meet the specific needs in each category.

1. Catastrophic risk solutions

Many catastrophic event solutions take the form of insurance policies. It is critically important to address these large financial risks with insurance rather than personal assets or investments. Failing to do so can result in significant capital misallocations. Depending on the client's specific situation, term-life, disability, long-term care, and umbrella policies may make sense. With other forms of insurance such as home and auto, there may be gaps that can be filled that can protect a client's assets.

2. Known liquidity solutions

The sole function of a known liquidity solution is to deliver a guaranteed stable value. This is typically delivered with a federally insured demand deposit account for amounts less than $250,000, or a cash-equivalent investment with immediate liquidity and low volatility for larger amounts. For more-complex situations, specific liabilities can be funded with investments such as Treasury or investment-grade bonds. In certain situations, accessing credit to fund unexpected or short-term liquidity also may be utilized to avoid untimely liquidation of assets and unnecessary tax burdens. The key point is to inventory specific items and assign values to determine concrete liquidity needs. Only investments with no or minuscule price volatility should be employed to meet known liquidity needs.

3. Regular income solutions

To meet regular income needs, an investment portfolio that generates reliable income on a regular basis should be the desired solution. It is critical that the portfolio's principal outpace inflation over time, so as not to lose its ability to generate a sufficient and growing income.

Often a sustainable distribution range, such as 4%, is set to inform portfolio construction and to set reasonable client expectations. With many investors living longer, incomes need to last much longer, too.

The portfolio should be constructed such that it produces a yield that can support a sustainable distribution rate. This ensures the principal can then be left untouched to target growth that outpaces inflation. With interest rates hovering around historic lows, advisors have had to look beyond traditional fixed income portfolios to deliver the necessary yield. Currently, high-yielding investments such as dividend-paying equities, real estate investment trusts, and master limited partnerships are well-suited for this need.

From a behavioral perspective, it is important for advisors to help clients separate the income stream and the principal value. For perspective, dividend research shows that 80–90% of dividend-paying companies keep dividends constant or increase them each year, which translates into a high level of confidence for the dividend stream. Meanwhile, the impact of stock volatility shrinks dramatically over longer time horizons. Separating the portfolio's income from its price variability can help to reduce client concerns about both short-term market volatility and the long-term risk of running out of money.

Only investments that can generate the required income reliably should be included in this portfolio.

4. Long-term capital growth solutions

Solutions in this arena should be tuned entirely for maximum capital appreciation over the long term. The most important factor should be expected returns, because the rate of return and compounding over time will dominate all other considerations. For this reason, the growth portfolio should be invested in equities. With a little research, high-quality active management can be identified to potentially add significant value, providing as much as 4–6% in excess returns over time.

Based on our research and that of others, equity strategies provided by actively managed mutual funds that meet the following criteria have the greatest chance to outperform over the long-run:

- Pursuing a narrowly defined strategy with consistency and conviction.

- Managing less than $1bn in a single strategy.

- Not closely tracking an index (R-squared below 0.80).

Constructing an equity portfolio of three to five truly active managers who pursue different strategies enhances the client's ability to stay invested over time by allowing different strategies to perform in different market environments.

We believe investments that have low expected return, or which place volatility reduction before capital appreciation, have no place in client growth portfolios.

5. Estate and legacy solutions

The estate and legacy areas are focused on intelligent divestiture of the client's wealth in accordance with the client's wishes. Because no two clients will be alike in this area, tailored solutions will be the norm.

Estate-planning and tax expertise can be leveraged effectively to create trusts, foundations, and charitable structures that help clients make a personal and meaningful impact with their lifetime of hard work.

Advisors should compile and maintain inventories of financial assets, where they are held, account numbers, how they are titled, and beneficiaries. This provides a complete financial picture and can be an invaluable resource when unexpected life events occur.

Step 4: Ongoing support

Figure 2.8 summarizes the full BWA process. We have discussed the activities in the first two circles; we now focus on the ongoing behavioral support that is a hallmark of the BWA.

Figure 2.8: Behavioral wealth management

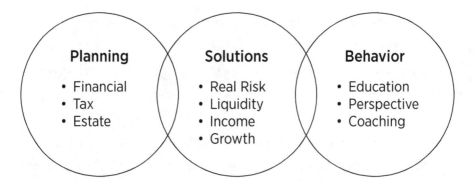

Measuring progress against goals

Ongoing management of the client's financial life requires organization, discipline, and communication. The communication process is an important part of managing client behaviors, particularly as it aligns with the client's behavioral profile and the expectations set at the outset.

Although the type of communication may vary, we recommend several meetings during each calendar year as an ongoing check-in to measure progress.

The face-to-face meeting provides a touchpoint for the ongoing relationship. Being well-prepared and organized can help to further the advisor's credibility. It is also an opportunity to review the plan and progress, to reinforce that maintaining the plan is just as important as its creation. The meeting should allow some time for free-form discussion as part of the greeting, but otherwise it should be well structured, with an agenda and a checklist of items to review.

The following are some specific recommendations to help guide the discussion and continue to manage client expectations as you report the performance of the financial plan:

- Measure progress toward client goals, rather than performance. Was liquidity met, income provided, and growth achieved?

- View results since the beginning of the relationship to show the cumulative difference you are making.

- Break out contributions, withdrawals, and capital appreciation (since inception and into the future) to illustrate how client choices are important drivers of outcomes.

Life events and adjustments

The checklist for every meeting should include a review and update of any life events or changes to the client's financial circumstances and goals. Advisors need a well-defined process whereby each major area of the plan is updated and reviewed at predetermined meetings to avoid trying to cover too much in a single sitting. This also will allow for specialists handling other parts of the financial plan to be included. Some common groupings are provided in Figure 2.9.

Figure 2.9: Events/*Checklists*/Inventories

Financial Plans	Risk Assessment	Inventory
• Liquidity Plan	• Life Insurance	• Accounts
• Income Plan	• Liability Insurance	• Titles
• Tax Projections	• Disablility	• Beneficiaries

Ongoing behavioral guidance

Educating clients and providing behavioral coaching is an ongoing process. Many parts of the client service model are designed to manage client behaviors, but likely will not be apparent to the client. There may be opportunities to point out specific actions and activities that are behavioral-centric in design, reinforcing to the client the important goal of managing behavioral biases. For example, the needs-based plan is a perfect opportunity to reinforce that its design is intended to help the client disregard the volatility that often triggers emotional selling.

Because a BWA is differentiated by this type of guidance, we also suggest providing timely communication geared to helping clients recognize common emotional triggers to avoid. A growing number of resources are available to help advisors and their clients gain a deeper understanding of how behavior shapes the investing landscape. One such example, among many, is Syntoniq, a software package that allows advisers to better measure the emotions that drive client behaviors.

Finally, Figure 2.10 is a graphical representation of the behavioral client experience the BWA is attempting to create.

Figure 2.10: The BWA client experience

Chapter review and what is to come

Behavioral wealth advising is an ongoing process with concrete behavioral elements and deliverables. The comprehensive needs-based plan is the foundation of the BWA service model because it builds control, confidence, and comfort that helps clients manage emotional triggers. Redefining risk beyond the mistaken use of volatility is also critical to making the transition.

Behavioral education and coaching occur throughout the overall service model. That coaching will help the client understand how a BWA is helping them avoid destructive behaviors and follow their long-term plans. The result will be more-satisfied clients, better client retention, and additional referrals.

The behavioral wealth advisor and supporting experts are members of the team helping clients gain confidence in their financial situation as well as build long-horizon wealth. While they seem to operate in quite different arenas, they are heavily dependent on one another. The BWA provides comprehensive planning and behavioral coaching that gives clients the confidence to invest in truly active funds.

In the following chapters we discuss how behavioral concepts can be applied to the various aspects of investment management.

Chapter 3.
Prescriptions for the Equity Investment Process

Overwhelmed

Wanting Yang was on information overload. She had successfully mastered the process of gathering and synthesizing information in her graduate program, but as a new mutual fund buy-side analyst, her information fire hose had grown many times larger.

She received numerous reports each day from sell-side analysts and others who sent their research on the economy, stock ideas, bond ideas, new portfolio management techniques, technical analysis, and on and on. How could she ever find the time to keep up with all of this information? Not only that, how could she begin to discern what was useful information? It seemed every last bit of information came from a reliable source, but which of it was important for her as an analyst?

Complicating this effort, Wanting wondered how the economic and market assumptions she was taught in graduate school could be taken seriously. Everyone she knew was motivated by the quirks of their psychology, not by pure rationality. Worse still, Wanting was aware that she needed to find a way to manage her own biases if she was to perform as close as possible to her best.

The great puzzle

These questions weighed heavily on Wanting. How does she go about the job of sorting information in order to extract useful signals from the background noise that is the news? How could she increase the quality of her own performance evaluation to ensure her investment process was sound? How could she keep her skill set current and, in the process, determine what was no longer necessary? And last, how could she overcome her own behavioral biases to minimize mistakes and risks, while maximizing successes and returns? Wanting believed that the answer to each of these questions centered around mastery of her own behavior.

Wanting had a deeply felt desire to be among the very best analysts at her firm and took seriously her fiduciary responsibility of being the custodian of her clients' dreams. She also wanted to perform well so that someday she would be promoted to fulfill her dream of becoming a mutual fund portfolio manager at her current firm or elsewhere.

Wanting felt intimidated by the amount of time and effort it was going to take in order to demonstrate her skills to herself, first, to her firm, second, and most importantly, to fund investors. With these thoughts in mind, Wanting set about creating her own unique equity investment process.

Minimizing our behavioral biases

Wanting's questions and concerns above are shared by most research analysts and investment decision-makers. It is a tacit recognition that minimizing the behavioral bias in our own investment process is one of the surest ways of improving our results, which of course requires the development of our own new habits and behaviors. Admittedly, this can be difficult. But the lack of ease in changing our behaviors means that if we succeed then we have an advantage over our competition, who are left to struggle with their biases.

Three useful skills for minimizing our behavioral biases in the investment process are improving our abilities to: filter information; measure our opinions and conclusions about information; and gain focus and awareness about our thinking. These three areas are the subject of the rest of this chapter.

How to read the news

A central theme of *ROAM* is that people are biased. If you accept this, then so too must journalists and other information providers be biased. Most investment decisions are based on information, much of which comes from third party sources, like the news. Therefore, a key issue for every investment professional is how to compensate for the behavioral biases inherent in the information they digest.

An analogy that may prove useful is to think of information and our understanding of it as a mosaic. Here, each new piece of information is equivalent to a tile in the overall mosaic. As we lay down more and more tiles our minds begin to create connections between the different parts of the mosaic. In this manner, pictures begin to emerge from the information. Not only that, but we can also see how individual pictures themselves relate to still other pictures in an overall narrative.

Jason solves the problem of how to eliminate bias in information by reading over 60 news sources each day, and sometimes even over 80 depending on how much time he has. This may sound daunting, but he doesn't read the news the way most people do. Jason starts with a premise: he is reading to eliminate his ignorance. That means that he does not read every article in those 60–80+ sources. Instead he reads the headlines and sub-headlines only. If Jason encounters a headline that he cannot relate to his knowledge mosaic, only then does he read the entire story. He does this, in part, because he knows the story is always bigger than the newspaper and/or the reporter. Put another way, there are always many sides to every story. By reading 60–80+ sources in a day he gets a bird's eye view of a story. This technique was developed in response to the problem Jason faced early in his career: the information fire hose is impossible for one person to drink in its entirety.

First, if a story is especially important globally then it is a headline for many different news sources. This ubiquity of coverage is a strong indication as to what the public likely finds important, because editors and publishers have featured the story widely.

Second, this approach also helps to control for the bias of editors and reporters. If a story is globally relevant, then by reading the story in multiple news outlets it is easier for Jason to see the angle of each paper and its reporters. This way the reader can pick up the preferred contextualizations and the specific details that were considered important, but that were left out in other sources. By considering many different accounts of the same story it also means that a fuller picture of the news may emerge.

Third, Jason intentionally reads papers and sources that he knows have an angle. He then complements that reading by trying to find another source that has the opposite, or very different angle. For example, on the day following the UK's referendum vote on membership of the European Union, every business paper in the world featured it as a story. The way it was covered in the UK's *Financial Times* was very different to how it was covered in *China Daily*.

Fourth, Jason tries to read primary sources when available. If there is data of interest referenced in an article, he tries to track down the source to see if the reporter fairly represents the underlying research. Surprisingly, the data is often not accurately represented!

This technique of reading the news is one way to help filter out the biases of individual reporters and to better ensure the information used in investment analysis is also less biased.

How to increase the objectivity of your performance evaluation

Absolutely essential to the return of active investment management success is tracking and overcoming your own behavioral biases. Another key skill is having a means of ensuring you are not just getting lucky. Here are several techniques designed to contend with these obstacles to success.

Opinion diaries

In the early days of Jason's investment career, he was anxious because he needed to know a critical thing: was he good at his job, or not? Investment professionals are constantly digesting and interpreting the news to ensure they understand things like GDP, corporate earnings, discounted cash flow analysis, technological trends, demographic shifts, and so forth. How is success at this activity measured? Overwhelmingly, it is not measured.

One day Jason realized in an Aha! moment that the returns of the fund he served as a research analyst did not reflect all of his decisions. Instead, the portfolio's returns only reflected the results of the securities he recommended and that were chosen for purchase by his boss. Another way to think about it: the portfolio returns directly reflected only a very small number of the affirmative – "buy that!" – decisions he made.

What about all of the companies that are bypassed for analysis and recommended purchase because they do not fit a thesis, or that did not pass muster after modeling of their futures? What about all of the management teams with whom you speak, that fail to assuage your concerns and convince you they deserve your shareholders' hard-earned capital? What about your failures, near misses, and weighting errors? What about the emotions that distort your decision-making? And on, and on. As investors we make thousands of decisions about our understanding of reality, and the portfolio returns track only a small minority of these decisions. Returns are nice, but they are clearly feedback on only a very minor subset of an investors' full decision suite.

Jason realized that to fulfill his aspiration of becoming a good investor he needed to record, date, and consistently examine a much higher percentage of his decisions in an opinion diary. Jason could then check in occasionally to examine to what degree his understanding of issues was in accord with reality. This turns out to be one of the most powerful of all investing secrets because it provides an ongoing and objective record of the inner workings of your mind, so long as you revisit the opinion diary as a check on the quality of your mind and its analyses.

Warning! You need to be unabashed and courageous in examining your failings. You also must have the courage and energy to craft answers to the questions raised when you review your opinion diary. Admitting our failings is very difficult, as behavioral finance tells us. Even if we admit our failings, we need courage and ingenuity to create solutions to our errors in process or judgment. Last, you have to muster the courage needed to change. Rarely is this fun, but almost always it is a source of betterment, and ultimately of investment success.

Here is one way to set up an opinion diary.

Record your important ideas and decisions in an opinion diary. This could be an e-document, or a written document.

Include the who, what, where, when, why, and how of your investment decisions. Pay particular attention to your emotional state at the time of the decisions.

Review your opinion diary at least quarterly and also whenever a major change in a decision occurs, such as a purchase, sale, or when an investment requires a major decision (e.g., merger or acquisition, CEO change, earnings announcements, etc.).

What sorts of decisions qualify for inclusion in the opinion diary? Anything that occupies your mind for a length of time so that you find yourself thinking about it, or returning to it.

For example, from Jason's career an entry in his opinion diary was made when Hugo Chavez, the former leader of Venezuela, ejected the foreign oil well engineers from the country. Jason believed that this would only affect Venezuela at some distant future date so there was no way to invest in this idea in any meaningful way for the foreseeable future. What he wrote circa 2002 was: "Chavez kicks out oil engineers. Their wells are sour [full of Sulphur] sludge… will kill their only source of wealth = eventual chaos."[47]

Likewise, your thoughts about the direction of the market over the next several months is also valid material for an opinion diary. Key is to notice how much mental space is taken up by a thought; especially record the persistent thoughts.

In summary, opinion diaries, because they are a record of your thoughts, provide a method to objectively assess the quality of your thinking, and to gain transparency into any behavioral biases from which you may suffer. For example:

- *Loss aversion* – checking in with your opinion diary allows you to see any excessive pessimism you have. Is pessimism a bias for you?

- *Overconfidence* – "I called that market development months ago," when, in fact, a check with the diary shows your opinion was very different.

- *Confirmation bias* – "Yes, the business failed to compete with the industry leader again this quarter, but I added more because it's cheap."

- *Herding* – Is there a persistent tone of excitement about market gyrations – both the bull and bear varieties – logged in your diary?

---

[47] See Robert Rapier, 'How Venezuela Ruined Its Oil Industry', *Forbes* (7 May 2017) for an overview of this sad story.

- *Anchoring* – Are you fixated on a particular issue? Or, do you tend to fixate on a narrow set of issues?

- *Availability* – Are your assessments differentiated from the information sources that inspired your thinking, or are you just responding to information written by others but that was in near proximity to you?

- *Representativeness* – Are your opinion diary entries stereotypical and comprised of investing heuristics, like: "Stocks climb a wall of worry," "Sell in May, and go away," "Bulls and bears make money on Wall Street, but hogs get slaughtered," and so on? If they contain these kinds of trite comments then chances are you are not thinking deeply enough.

- *Mental accounting* – Is your thinking unnecessarily compartmentalized?

Investment thesis

Wouldn't it be nice to know the questions to ask of a business's management before investing? Wouldn't it be nice to have such an excellent understanding of a business that when you read the news you actually have an understanding of how that news might affect the business? Wouldn't it be nice to know the criteria that are legitimate reasons to sell your interest in a business? Wouldn't it be nice to make investment decisions freer from emotion? These are among the most difficult things for investors to apprehend. But one tool helps with all of them: the investment thesis.

The investment thesis is a contractual document you write to outline the relationship between you and your investment. Just like all contracts, the investment thesis provides the grounds for evaluating the relationship in an objective, legal-like fashion. Because you are the only witness to this agreement you must respect the investment thesis with sanctity. This means that if an investment violates the investment thesis that you have created then you will agree to sell it, rather than rationalizing a continued reason to own it. This is a key technology for helping you to overcome multiple behavioral biases (as above), but especially:

- Confirmation

- Anchoring

- Availability

- Representativeness

Here are the key elements to include in your investment thesis:

- Name of the investment

- Current date

- *Investment time horizon*, or alternatively, how long do you expect this business to contribute desirable returns to your portfolio.

- Strengths of the business:

- *Duration of strength* – for each strength include an estimate for how long you believe each strength might be in place. For example, if you feel that the business has a dominant product, write down how many years you feel this product will be dominate.

- *Strength devil's advocate* – imagine ways that the strengths could be overcome by competition or pure chance.

- Weaknesses of the business:

  - *Duration of weakness* – for each weakness include an estimate for how long you believe each weakness might be in place.

  - *Weakness devil's advocate* – imagine ways that the weaknesses could be overcome by management efforts or pure chance.

- *Anxieties* about the business

- *Ignorance* about the business – the parts of the business you want to understand better.

- *Why you feel like buying* – the emotions, not the data, behind your decision.

- *Definite selling triggers* – things that would cause you to sell the investment immediately.

- *Possible selling triggers* – things that might cause you to sell the investment immediately.

If you end up buying an interest in the business, record on your investment thesis the following:

- Price you paid for the investment

- Date of purchase

Now you have a contract between the current you and the future you. Because so many of the behavioral biases are about a lack of memory, or a denial of memory (i.e., a rationalization), having a record of why you purchased an investment provides a level of objectivity for you in the future.

Investment theses are living documents and must be updated to reflect new and critical information that affects your contract. Vitally, this does not grant you the power to radically change your thesis to serve as a means to justify any emotional connection you have to an investment.

Lessons learned

It is all too tempting to bury our heads in the sand after one of our investments loses money. But these failures are a rich opportunity to get better. A helpful attitude is to accept that mistakes are a part of active investment management and that your goal is to never repeat the same mistake.

The tool for accomplishing this is the lessons learned list. This is a post-mortem of the causes of the investment loss. What key factors did you not appreciate? What errors in judgment occurred? What biases clouded your assessment?

As an example, earlier in Jason's career he invested in Premier Parks (the ticker was PKS at the time), the owner of Six Flags amusement parks. His investment essentially went sideways for many years, never really going up, or down. Yes, there would be periods when the stock performed well, but then extended periods when it would not. Despite being a well-managed business, the reason for the sideways movement was that the operating period for Premier Parks was extremely limited. Most of the amusement parks were only open from the end of May through to the end of September, and with intensity in earned revenues in June through August. Further, the business was also very susceptible to poor weather patterns. If bad weather swept through the Northeastern region of the US then Premier Parks attendance was negatively affected. Here is a quote from Jason's Lessons Learned list:

> "The window of opportunity for a seasonal business's stock price to appreciate is the length of their operating season. After the operating season the stock is dead money. Perhaps more important to recognize, the shortened window of opportunity amplifies any bad news for a seasonal business. For while the size of the rock that hits the pond is the same size as for a non-seasonal business, the pond it hits is much smaller so the ripples are larger. Example: When PKS has bad news the magnitude is always disproportionate to its relevance."

Continuous curiosity

Understanding information is crucial to success as an investor which means, all other things being equal, the investment pro who understands information the best wins more than those that do not. It is also true, though, that the investment pro who understands the most information also wins more than those that do not. So, what is the behavior that drives someone to constantly search out new experiences, new perspectives, and new ways of doing things, and to constantly expand past her personal boundaries to understand more information? It is curiosity. Curiosity is the constant urge to explore what lies at our personal frontiers and thus is the fuel for becoming more knowledgeable, and likely better.

To be curious also implies eagerness to learn and to change. News flow, the raw data of the investment business, is constantly changing and demanding that we learn new things. Thus, an investment manager possessed of curiosity mostly finds the constant flow of information is a wonderful thing. Yes, there are times when the news flow overwhelms, but the curious investment manager mostly feels enriched by their encounters with the ever-changing world. In turn, this provides longevity in the business.

Furthermore, curious investment managers are not easily satisfied. Instead, they constantly seek out more information, new understanding, and new skills. Their curiosity also leads them to question more, and to seek out their own answers rather than settling for conventional wisdom.

Let your ignorance guide you

Curiosity is about a willingness to explore what lies on the other side of your personal boundaries. Naturally, then, curiosity requires us to have knowledge of those personal boundaries. Ask yourself, do you exit the comfort of what you know frequently by seeking out new perspectives, or new ideas? If not, start to notice when you feel ignorant about a subject and let that feeling be the spark driving your research interests.

In other words, it may be that standing in the way of your curiosity is a fear of feeling ignorant. The antidote is simply to get more information.

Personal knowledge inventory

Another idea is to take a personal knowledge inventory. Begin by writing down those things or skills that you know a lot about. After that, list the things you know something about, but for which you may not be an expert. Next, list things for which you have only a passing amount of knowledge. Choose something from your list where your knowledge is only passing, or for which additional knowledge would make you an expert. The personal knowledge inventory lays bare your knowledge spectrum and allows you to cross into your knowledge frontier.

Honor your curiosity

If you believe that you are naturally curious but haven't been lately, then honor your innate quality. If topics of interest lay unexplored, then follow the flame of interest that curiosity provides, even if it seems unrelated to investing. For example, you may have a curiosity about Frederick the Great but because this seems only loosely related to investing you have not read a biography about the man. Yet, it may turn out that something in Frederick's understanding of the world helps you to understand something in investing. It could be how Frederick approached problem-solving, or it could be that it helps you better understand the geopolitics of France and Germany that, in turn, helps you better understand the EU.

Gaining focus and awareness of our thinking

A central theme of *ROAM* is that behavioral finance is largely a diagnosis lacking prescriptions. Worse still, many of the promulgators of behavioral finance talk about behavioral biases being hardwired when, in fact, our ability to learn and change courtesy of our neuroplasticity is more salient. The reason that behavioral biases are difficult to overcome isn't because we are doomed by our biology to commit errors in judgment, it is because:

- We rarely have spent time training our minds to reflect on our decision-making.

- Habits are difficult to change.

An understanding of the major behavioral biases allows us to state that they stem, not from our biology, but from our lack of development of our neurology. Said another way, we have a lack of conscious awareness of how our minds function. We can think of improving our consciousness as a hardware upgrade of the mind; a different kind of ROAM, a return to active mentation. Hereafter, our software – knowledge, skills, and abilities – also operates better. The good news is that improving our consciousness is a hallmark of a meditation practice. Specifically, there are two main skills to practice and attain:

1. Metacognition – awareness of awareness itself.

2. Top-down control – this is the ability to choose what to think and when to think it.

When someone has both metacognition and top-down control, behavioral biases are more easily overcome, as research has demonstrated on multiple occasions.[48] This research has directly pitted those who have just recently learned meditation (eight weeks of education) against those who do not know meditation in classic games used to identify behavioral bias (e.g. the ultimatum game). The result is that meditators, depending on the circumstance, are between 50–100% less biased. There is still bias present, but the effects are ameliorated. Meditation has also been shown to overcome other biases like ageism and racism.[49]

It is outside the scope of our book to provide you with a full training manual, but it is easy to sketch out two major forms of meditation that directly train the above abilities of metacognition and top-down control.

Open-monitoring trains metacognition

We are certain that you have heard much about mindfulness and mindfulness meditation. A common misunderstanding is that mindfulness and meditation are the same thing; they are not. Formally, mindfulness is a commonly-used term for what psychologists and neuroscientists call open-monitoring meditation. This form of meditation is scientifically demonstrated to improve your metacognition. Because metacognition is awareness of awareness itself, it allows meditators to better track the content of their thoughts, and

---

[48] Ulrich Kirk, Jonathan Downar, P. Read Montague, 'Interoception drives increased rational decision-making in meditators playing the ultimatum game', *Frontiers in Neuroscience* 5 (April 2011), pp. 1–11 and Ulrich Kirk, Xiaosi Gu, Ann H. Harvey, Peter Fonagy, P. Read Montague, 'Mindfulness training modulates value signals in ventromedial prefrontal cortex through input from insular cortex', *NeuroImage* 100 (2014), pp. 254–262.

[49] Adam Lueke, Bryan Gibson, 'Mindfulness Meditation Reduces Implicit Age and Race Bias: The Role of Reduced Automaticity of Responding', *Social Psychological and Personality Science* (2014), pp. 1–8.

in real time. Clearly this has benefits for overcoming behavioral biases, because the biases are the inability to monitor the way that you are thinking.

The steps of a simple mindfulness meditation are as follows:

1. Remove yourself from unwanted distractions such as email or your smart device. Hint: you can inform your co-workers you are going to try to practice meditation. Or, wait until you have some private time to try.

2. Get yourself comfortable by either sitting in a favorite chair or on a favorite sofa.

3. Intentionally begin to take deep breaths in order to relax yourself. Do this until you start to relax.

4. Gradually stop controlling your breathing and ease into normal, relaxed breathing.

5. Now turn your attention to the contents of your mental activity. Most of us have many kinds of thoughts, incomplete thoughts, sensory information, judgments, and so on, coursing through our minds.

6. Rather than following any of this mental activity, instead notice its occurrence and contents; do not judge the contents in any way; and then let the thought disappear from consciousness as it naturally would do on its own.

7. Now return your attention to noticing the contents of your mind. Again, as activity arises, notice the content, do not judge the content, and then let them slip away as if they were feathers on a stream.

8. It is likely that your mind will wander at times as you follow the thoughts. Do not judge yourself as this is a natural occurrence. Once you have noticed the mind wandering, return your attention to the open-monitoring of your thoughts.

The above open-monitoring meditation can be done for as little as three to five minutes at first, but see if you can develop the ability to meditate in this way for 10–15 minutes per day, for five days a week. In so doing you will begin to develop your metacognitive abilities.

Focused attention trains top-down control

The ability to choose what to think and when you think it helps to overcome behavioral bias because you can choose to focus your attention on the contents of your mind (the skill cultivated by open-monitoring meditation). Above, the primary difficulty of an open-monitoring meditation is mind-wandering, which a focused attention meditation helps to overcome once the mind's attention function is improved. By contrast, a focused attention meditation without an open-monitoring practice can result in too much focus on a single thing, and not enough noticing.

Here are the steps for a focused attention meditation (the first four steps are the same as for open-monitoring meditation above):

1. Remove yourself from unwanted distractions such as email or your smart device. Hint: you can inform your co-workers you are going to try to practice meditation. Or, wait until you have some private time to try.

2. Get yourself comfortable by either sitting in a favorite chair or on a favorite sofa.

3. Intentionally begin to take deep breaths in order to relax yourself. Do this until you start to relax.

4. Gradually stop controlling your breathing and ease into normal, relaxed breathing.

5. Now as your mind inevitably begins to wander, first, notice that your mind has wandered, and then gently return your attention to the simple rhythm of your breath; the inhale… and the exhale… of your breath.

6. Each time your mind wanders, gently return your attention to the natural rhythm of the inhale and exhale of your breath.

A focused attention meditation can also be done for as little as three to five minutes at first, but see if you can develop the ability to meditate in this way for 10–15 minutes per day, for five days a week. In so doing you will begin to develop your top-down control abilities. A powerful meditation process to improve your ability to naturally overcome behavioral bias is to practice both a focused attention and open-monitoring meditation. Dedicating 30 minutes per day to meditation may sound like a lot of time, but because of its demonstrable benefits for improving mental function, this cost is more than made up for by its benefits.

Additional meditation benefits (outside the scope of this book) include lower stress; improved overall health; improved mental functioning, including better memory and creativity; and improved ethics.

Now, here is a guide to behavioral finance's major biases and how meditation may help to overcome them.

How meditation helps overcome behavioral biases

Loss aversion bias

With loss aversion bias we feel the pain of loss approximately twice as acutely as we do the pleasure from gain. In other words, for most people their default trigger is to try to avoid personal harm or loss. Active investment management is essentially an anxiety-inducing machine, with its volatile financial markets, unexpected geopolitical occurrences, surprises from our investments, and so on. In other words, investing is a loss-aversion button pusher.

On the good news front, many studies prove that meditation lowers stress and increases awareness. What this means is that instead of having our deliberate thinking subsumed by loss aversion in stressful moments, meditating investors can take advantage of these times and calmly buy when everyone else is selling.

Overconfidence bias

If you have served as an active investment professional for any length of time, surely you have noticed that having your securities rise in value can lead to feelings of elation, yes? This is all well and good, so long as it does not also lead to overconfidence. This bias can lead to outsized risks being taken or analysis being ignored. Here the non-judgmental self-awareness of meditators allows investment pros to notice their feelings of invincibility and to monitor their emotions in real time.

Confirmation bias

Man-with-a-hammer syndrome, alias confirmation bias, is looking for and focusing on information that affirms the point of view we already hold about something. Another expression of confirmation bias is rationalization. Here, even if a business is performing worse than our expectations we can find something – such as, "Morgan Stanley is maintaining their buy rating" – that allows us to hold our thesis as sacrosanct. At the core though, this is an inability to separate our preferences and prejudices from the facts; it is a denial of reality. Again, meditation allows people to examine their thoughts in real time. If you couple this awareness with a willingness to learn a new way of responding to the world then confirmation bias can be overcome.

Herding bias

Hopefully we have convinced you that most financial market volatility is the result of emotions. This is especially true during periods of very wide swings when more investors than typical all act in the same way, and most typically in reaction to bad news. Because meditation allows active investment managers to examine the content of their thoughts in an objective way, using focused metacognition, it is possible in these moments to evaluate the wisdom of the herd response. It could be that the response is entirely logical, and if so, that a sell in the face of bad news is appropriate. It is more often the case, though, that herding is an emotional and irrational response to news. By gaining the ability to monitor the source of our own mental activity, we can assess whether or not we are emotionally reacting, or deliberately responding. Thus, meditation is a powerful antidote to herding bias.

Anchoring bias

Anchoring bias means that we tend to place undue emphasis on data that is presented to us first. An example is that if in an investment committee meeting the value of a business is first put forth as £55 per share, the final value agreed to is most likely anchored on that first estimate. Another example might be taking the fair value estimate or target price from a sell-side research firm as the first take in our assessment. Meditation allows us to notice when mentally we are conducting research relative to information presented to us first. In these moments we can stop the mental cascade, slow down, and actually research the facts needed to assess a situation independent of an anchor. One final and classic example of anchoring is not selling shares in a company until they again ascend above our cost basis. This is known as a sunk cost. What was paid for the security is irrelevant. Instead, what matters is what the prices are worth now based on the perceived future prospects for the issuer.

Availability bias

This distorted thinking is very similar to anchoring bias, where we rely upon a preferred information source, or a common information source, to make an assessment. For example, if our preferred source for business news is the *Financial Times*, we may rely upon their version of a story about a company or event in Southeast Asia rather than going to a news source where the journalist was on the ground. Overcoming the temptation of availability bias requires that we do not react to an event in our default manner, and instead go out of our way to surface the truth of a story. Meditation once more can help us place a much-needed awareness-pause between stimulus and reaction/response.

Representativeness bias

Representativeness bias is essentially assessing new situations based on stereotypes. So, when we hear a pitch at a sell-side event for a waste company, we tend to ignore the specific details and instead relate the presentation to our previous experience with garbage businesses. If we have lost money in garbage companies previously then it is significantly likely that we cannot see the current garbage company in a fair light.

For most of us, just before our mental model kicks in, there is a check-in with our memory: "What story do I know that is similar to this one?" Then there is a moment of cognition or connection to our memory. Meditators can tune into and become aware of the feeling of cognition. Then, when evaluating a new company, rather than fall prey to representativeness bias, meditators can interrupt the activation of the mental model when they feel it being activated: "Waste Company B really is different from Waste Company A."

Mental accounting bias

Classically, mental accounting bias is a compartmentalizing of money into different categories to which we apply different decision rules. We may not sell a fully valued stock because it is part of a falsely defined category we have created within a portfolio that we call "growth capital." For this part of the portfolio we have a decision-rule of, "growth can sometimes be very overvalued." Instead, to raise cash we may sell a security with better prospects that we believe is a part of the "value capital" in the fund.

This kind of behavioral bias is the inability to break context or consider multiple contexts before making a decision. Again, meditation emphasizes unbiased, present-moment states of consciousness. As meditators get better they can hear themselves think, and avoid needlessly narrowing their contexts of understanding while maintaining a more holistic worldview.

* * *

In conclusion, a skillful meditation practice allows investors to choose their contexts, mental models, and actions with greater awareness and non-judgment. Each of these abilities provides tools for overcoming the biases identified by behavioral finance. In fact, meditation has been helping people think more clearly and with greater awareness for 3000 years: 75 times longer than the 40-year history of behavioral finance.

Software as a behavioral complement

Many in the active investment community fear not only the constant march toward 0% fees, but also the rise of AI-enabled investment managers, which could make people obsolete. Less widely covered is the software that has been developed to aid the active investment managers in their quest to overcome their own behavioral biases.

One such example is Syntoniq, a firm whose software provides a sophisticated series of tests authored by behavioral finance professors to assess your behavioral biases. Additionally, the software identifies which of your biases is likely hurting you the most and hence critical to your success to correct.

Another firm, Essentia Analytics, asks its subscribers to upload their historical trade data. This information is then analyzed by sophisticated algorithms, as well as former portfolio managers service as coaches, to offer up insight into your behavioral biases. Interestingly, the software also provides warnings when you are about to engage in behaviors that have hurt your performance in times past.

Falling in love with stocks

A recent Essentia paper by Chris Woodcock, Aleasi Rowland, and Snežana Pejić, entitled 'The Alpha Lifecyle', provides evidence of what many think is the case: managers fall in love with their stocks and end up hurting returns by selling too late. Figure 3.1 presents their main results.

Figure 3.1: Grand mean of cumulative return on ROI over all stock time episodes

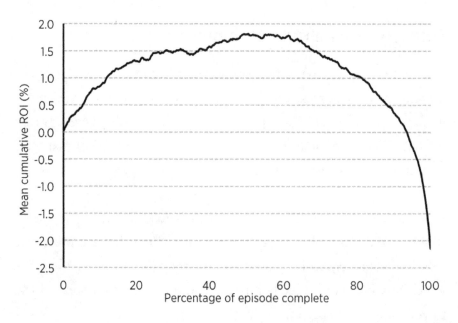

Note: Based on 10,000 holdings (episodes) for 43 equity portfolios over the period 2006–2019. Each holding period is standardized to range from 0 to 100% of days held. ROI is the cumulative net alpha divided by the amount invested in the stock at that time. Reprinted with permission of Essentia Analytics.

The initial upward slope reveals the average manager displays stock picking talent and this skill contributes to increasing alpha, up to about 50% to 60% of the holding period. After that, alpha begins to decline and plummets to negative territory during the last 5% of the holding period. That is, on average managers fall in love with their stocks and hold to the point of extinguishing the hard-earned initial alpha. Managers would significantly benefit by learning to sell a stock before this final destructive chapter.

Developing a rules-based selling rule is one of the most important emotional adjustments a manager can make to an investment process.

Chapter review and what is to come

In this chapter we discussed various ways to improve the investment process to rid it of behavioral bias. These included ways of reading the news to better ensure we see more of the story, as well as ways of better ensuring our own objectivity when digesting the world's happenings.

Next we provided several additional methods of ensuring our objectivity, including the power of opinion diaries, and investment theses. Curiosity is also an essential behavior for drawing us into the unknown. By indulging our curiosity, we slowly improve our knowledge, and consequently it is likely that we improve our investment process, too. Last, we shared the importance of meditation as a scientifically proven way for overcoming behavioral bias.

Chapter 4 is a deep dive into the many ways in which behavior and behavioral insights may be utilized in fundamental analysis.

Chapter 4.
Prescriptions for Fundamental Analysis

Art of investment analysis

WANTING YANG WAS beginning to get her feet under her as a young mutual fund analyst. She was currently conducting research on a company whose securities were added to the fund prior to her hiring. The fund is one of the top ten largest shareholders for this company.

Wanting thought that this stature should give her access to the company's executives so that any questions she had would be answered by them. In particular, she was concerned that the business was no longer selling competitive products and that its golden era of success may be ending. To alleviate her concerns, she wanted to question the chief financial officer or investor relations professional to get a detailed explanation of the new strategy announced by management in order to restore its competitiveness.

Revealing behavior

Others at her fund are also interested in discussing the strategy with the company. Much to her surprise, they get the brush off from the chief financial officer. They then try to schedule a phone call with an investor relations executive. After many weeks of trying to schedule the call, she was finally able to get access.

About 15 minutes into the long-awaited conference call the investor relations professional cut short the questioning. He does this because his family has just gotten a new puppy and he needs to go home to walk the dog to avoid "an incident." This left Wanting and her colleagues a bit aghast, and without answers to crucial questions.

Wanting, even as a young analyst, considered this to be hubris and a strong indication that the company did not take her fund and its shareholders seriously. A further analysis of the company's quantitative results matched to management's strategy and expectations for the firm confirmed that the company had lost its way. Stated another way, the company's bad behavior toward shareholders in direct interaction was important information, along with the quantitative results.

While disappointed that a company would treat her and her colleagues this way, it was the latest reminder to Wanting that behavior plays a key role in the careful analysis of an investment opportunity.

It's the behavior

ROAM postulates that human behavior is a better predictor of the movement of prices in financial markets than modern portfolio theory. That thesis may also be extended to the human behavior expressed by the management teams and employees of businesses. That is, we believe if you examine human behavior and come to an understanding about it, at the market level or the firm level, you can deliver results that are superior to those relying on less comprehensive analyses. Predominately, this is because behaviors, like habits, are hard to change.

In the anecdote above pitting Wanting against the firm she was evaluating, the behavior of its executives was indicative of a culture of condescension and disinterest in a crucial group of the firm's stakeholders: investors. Crucially, the firm under scrutiny needed investor buy-in if it was to improve its competitiveness and renew its growth trajectory.

This chapter discusses ways of using a behavioral lens to improve financial statement analysis, valuation, one-on-one management interviews, and quarterly earnings announcements.

Financial statement analysis

It is our experience that most research analysts think the data contained in financial statements like the income statement, balance sheet, and cash flow statement are purely quantitative. Most see this as the raw material for the most objective work they do as research analysts. We do not dispute the quantitative nature of the data contained within financial statements. Rather, we would ask for an addition to be made to the conversation. Namely, that financial statements are also evidence of the actions of the people at a business.

Income statement

What are revenues, but an expression of the behaviors of the organization with regard to product development, product sourcing, product manufacturing, product inventorying, product marketing, brand management, relationship management, and so on? In other words, revenues are the result of the choices of the organization. Behaviors are the cause, with revenues being the effect.

This is true for all other financial statement accounts, too, ranging from interest expense, to accrued other liabilities, to investing cash flows from disposal of assets. Each of the effects logged and recorded in these many and varied accounts is evidence of the behavior of the organization.

The income statement, for example, can also be thought of as the stakeholder statement, ordered from most important stakeholder, to the least important. Revenues record the behavior and result of the company's interactions with its customers. Costs of goods sold log the result of the company's interactions with its suppliers. Sales, general, and administrative log the result of an organization's behaviors with regard to its external marketers, advertising platforms, employees, consultants, business equipment lessors, and so on. Research and development expense measures the behaviors of the organization with regard to its future product development and to its research staff. Eventually, a research analyst, in her quest for understanding, comes to the operating income line.

Excepting revenues, the figures from cost of goods sold down to operating income is the quantitative expression of the actions/behaviors/choices/decisions/ethics (ABCDE) of the operations professionals, especially the chief operating officer, of a firm. How are these expenses fluctuating relative to the global economy? Relative to the operating environment of the firm's industry? Relative to the products of the firm? And so on. Each of these provide insight about the culture of the firm's operations.

If, for example, expenses are trending downward when similar expenses globally are trending upward, it may be behavioral evidence of a disciplined operating team focused on the nitty gritty of operating a business. It could also be evidence of a culture of tough negotiators who fight for every last cent to keep expenses low.

Continuing on down the income statement, we come to the behaviors that contribute to or subtract from the value of the organization from its financing function. Has the chief financial officer managed the yield curve well? How about the overall capital structure? Is it appropriate for the firm given its business and its strategy? Do they have too much leverage, not enough? Is their interest rate too high, or too low relative to their performance? Is the CFO sophisticated enough to add value by shopping for the correct tax jurisdiction?

Next, below the CFO portion of the income statement, are the one-time and exceptional items that are the result of past ABCDE on the part of management. A history of one-time and exceptional items is an indication of a management team that suffers either delusions of grandeur (the bar is set unrealistically high), or that cannot execute its ideas (the bar is incapable of being jumped).

Finally, at long last, research analysts come to the net income line and can evaluate the overall operating and stakeholder performance of the business. But embedded in each of those accounts is evidence of an ongoing narrative for the company. *What are the numbers saying?*

Balance sheet

Just as the income statement is a record of the ABCDE of management, so too is the balance sheet. Current assets like cash, accounts receivable, and inventory all are expressions of the operations of the company because they directly tie to revenues and the reason why the firm exists in the first place. If there is a change in these accounts that deviates too far from the revenue performance, what is the explanation? Is it external factors such as the overall economy, or the competitive environment? Or is it something internal, such as poor communications, poor morale among employees, or poor management? Further down the balance sheet's asset column, long-term assets such as property, plant, and equipment are especially the purview of the operations professionals, such as the cheif operating office (COO). Again, these are indications of the ABC of management.

On the right side of the balance sheet are the liabilities and the shareholders' equity sections. Liabilities, including those that are short-term in nature, are expressions of the ABCDE of the financing professionals at an organization. Crucial to understanding the financing quality of the business is an evaluation of the firm's capital structure. Is the amount of debt correct relative to the stability of the company's revenue performance and its operating expenses? Is the interest paid too high relative to the competition? Is the company relying on floating interest rate instruments in order to make its promised earnings growth?

A detailed assessment of the ABCDE of the financing part of the company requires exploration of the financial statement footnotes, as well. For example, the footnotes show the maturity schedule for debts. Does the company generate enough cash flow from operations that it can afford to retire debts about to mature? If not, then it will need to rollover that debt into a new instrument. Is this occurring at a time of high interest rates, or low interest rates? In other words, how well has the CFO managed the yield curve?

Footnotes can also answer the question about whether management improved the appearance of the efficiency of the business, as measured by the return on assets and return on equity, by off-loading key manufacturing assets into operating leases. To tell, read the operating lease (sometimes called commitments and contingencies) footnote to see if the equipment financed by the leases is key to the operations of the business.

Table 4.1 provides a recent example of capitalized operating leases from a publicly traded company, Protolabs (ticker: PRLB), and as compared to their revenues.

Table 4.1: Protolabs capitalized operating leases

	2014	2015	2016	2017	2018
Operating leases	$ 17,682	$ 26,210	$ 58,457	$ 64,432	$ 60,229
As % of revenues	9.8	6.7	8.8	17.0	14.5

Note the large increase in capitalized operating leases relative to revenues as a percentage starting at 8.8% in 2016 and rising to 17% in 2017. What does the firm say about the benefit provided to the business by these operating leases? If the leases do not pertain to a mission-critical part of the business, then management's ABCDE is in the clear.

"The Company leases property from third parties. The Company leases three of its U.S. facilities with terms expiring at various times from 2019 to 2022. The Company also leases office space in the United Kingdom, France, Germany, Sweden and Italy with terms expiring at various times from 2019 to 2025. The Company leases an office and *manufacturing space* in Japan, and the initial term expires in April 2023. The Company also leases *manufacturing space* in Germany with terms expiring at various times from 2019 to 2028 [emphasis ours]."

The revenues of the firm in question are earned by providing outsourced manufacturing for other companies. In other words, these leases for manufacturing space are, in fact, the beating heart of the business. If the company lost access to this space then it would certainly affect their operating results.

Also, because the financial statements are all interrelated, active investment managers must also adjust other accounts, too. The manufacturing firm above is renowned for being debt-free. Yet, as you can see above, the operating leases show 14.5% leverage in 2018.

Last, the company is also famous for its return on assets (ROA), but an important part of that story is missing unless capitalized operating leases are included in the total assets portion of the calculation (i.e., the denominator).

Table 4.2: Protolabs adjusted return on assets (ROA)

	2014	2015	2016	2017	2018
ROA (%)	16.1	14.4	11.0	11.1	13.5
ROA, adj. (%)	15.0	13.4	9.9	9.8	12.1
% Diff.	7.4	6.8	10.9	13.2	11.0

As you can see in Table 4.2, the firm's return on assets is too high by over 10% in the three most recent years. Why aren't the capitalized operating leases on the liabilities side of the balance sheet? Said directly, this fact demands that active investment managers stop and take note because it may be revealing of the ABCDE of the business, and especially of its financing professionals.

Other liabilities that need footnote examination to fully appreciate are pension obligations and the cost of options. Companies have higher amounts of discretion with these liabilities, and therefore they are rich sources of evaluating its ABCDE.

Cash flow statement

Of the three financial statements, the one that most directly ties to the different executive behaviors of the firm is the cash flow statement. This is because its three major sections are: operating cash flow (CEO/COO), investing cash flow (CEO/CFO/COO), and financing cash flow (CFO).

The representation of cash flows is straightforward, but one tip is to look at the volatility of the net working capital section of cash flows from operations, over time, and as compared with revenues. This section shows the actual operating volatility of the business despite the smoothing that can be done by management in the income statement.

Examples of smoothing (i.e., poor ABCDE) include share buybacks meant to make an earnings number, rather than being an investment in undervalued shares, the extension of credit to customers in order to induce purchases as shown by an increase in days sales outstanding, and so on.

We highly encourage you to begin to look at the financial statement accounts for each business in which you own securities and ask of yourself the question: which behaviors are being recorded here? What are the commitments being made by management with regard to these accounts? Is there a clear and logical pathway for how management intends to change its and the organizations' behavior to change the effects logged by these accounts?

What do you do with the above understanding about the behaviors logged and recorded in financial statements? How can it be made more useful?

Essential to understanding ABCDE is to compare the quantitative story of the business as logged and recorded in the financial statements with the qualitative narrative about the business told by management. By doing this, active investment managers can begin to turn the data of the financial statements into actionable information.

For example, if company management has discussed and made promises about its strategy for several years in its 'Management's Discussion & Analysis (MDA)' section then management's ability to deliver on its commitments to stakeholders may be evaluated. Management makes commitments about their business' prospective performance in other venues, too. These include at industry conferences, finance industry conferences, on earnings conference calls, on merger and acquisition conference calls, and in one-on-one meetings.

What we recommend research analysts do if they are interested in moving an evaluation of business behavior to the forefront of their fundamental analysis is to begin logging and recording the commitments made by management at industry conferences, on conference calls, or in their written presentations, including regulatory filings. Then as each quarter's results are published, compare the quantitative effects to the qualitative/behavioral causes.

Xerox case study

Let's look at an example of analysing management ABCDE from Jason's career, featuring Xerox (ticker: XRX). Jason ended up recommending a reduction in the Davis Appreciation & Income Fund's stake because management was stating as a part of its strategic plan in the heart of the dot.com era that it anticipated five consecutive years of 10%+ total revenue growth.

This was an incredible (literally without credibility) claim on the part of management because its best performance for revenue growth over the preceding many years was capped at 10% (see below, 1995), and that was in a year in which everything had gone right for the company. Furthermore, management could not provide a clear description of the strategic pathway for changing the organization's behaviors that were going to lead to different results.

Table 4.3 shows Xerox's total revenue performance 1993–1999.

Table 4.3: Xerox total revenue performance, $USm (1993–1999)

Revenues	1993	1994	1995	1996	1997	1998	1999
Sales	$7,211	$7,823	$8,750	$9,256	$9,881	$10,752	$10,346
Service & rentals	$5,954	$6,255	$6,830	$7,107	$7,257	$7,626	$7,856
Finance income	$1,064	$1,006	$1,008	$1,015	$1,006	$1,071	$1,026
Total Revenues	$14,229	$15,084	$16,588	$17,378	$18,144	$19,449	$19,228

And, in Table 4.4, the growth rates associated with the above revenue performance.

Table 4.4: Xerox revenue growth (1993–1999)

Revenues	1994	1995	1996	1997	1998	1999	Avg.	CAGR
Sales (%)	8.5	11.8	5.8	6.8	8.8	–3.8	6.3	6.2
Service & rentals (%)	5.1	9.2	4.1	2.1	5.1	3.0	4.8	4.7
Finance income (%)	–5.5	0.2	0.7	–0.9	6.5	–4.2	-0.5	–0.6
Total Revenues (%)	6.0	10.0	4.8	4.4	7.2	–1.1	5.2	5.1

Look at the revenue growth from 1993 to 1998, the year Jason decided Xerox's management's ABCDE was questionable. You can see that 1995 was their very best year, logging 10% revenue growth. The average per year growth was 6.5%, while the compound annual growth rate (CAGR) was 6.4%.

How was management going to coax 10% per year performance out of a photocopier business for the next five years? They could only do so by inducing people to print more, rather than sending digital scans of documents. Blood from a stone, and all that. This seemed unlikely because every person Jason knew was sending and receiving more PDF versions of documents and viewing them directly, not printing them.

Let's now fast forward one year to 1999 to examine how Xerox was doing in executing its five-year plan of 10% per year total revenue growth, and especially the behavior of management in response to its performance. Table 4.5 presents Xerox's discussion of major product categories from their 1999 SEC-mandated annual report, known as the 10-K.

Table 4.5: Xerox 10-K from 1999

Total Revenues	1997	1998	1999	ex. Brazil
Digital products (%)	25	36	18	22
Light-lens copiers (%)	–2	–11	–21	–18
Paper & other products (%)	3	1	1	2

Here is the excerpt from Xerox's 1999 10-K in their Management's Discussion & Analysis section, discussing their preceding year's performance:

"The digital product portfolio includes production publishing, production printing, color copying and printing, our expanding family of black-and-white Document Centre digital multi-function products and network laser printers sold through indirect channels. Excluding Brazil, digital product revenues grew 22% in 1999, driven by outstanding revenue growth from our expanding Document Centre family of products, excellent laser printer revenue growth, strong color copying and printing growth, good production publishing growth and relatively flat production printing revenue."

The above paragraph is an indication of management's lack of forthright behavior (bad ABCDE). Why? For starters, they are discussing their revenue performance for the year and this is a story that may be told directly via relating the numbers. Yet, there is only one quantity in the entire paragraph: 22%. That 22% figure appears in the paragraph where they are discussing their sexiest products. Yet, even this figure has been modified to show it in its best light. How did they arrive at the figure? Like so:

"To understand the trends in the business, we believe that it is helpful to adjust revenue and expense growth (except for ratios) to exclude the impact of changes in the translation of foreign currencies into U.S. dollars. We refer to this adjusted growth as 'pre-currency growth'."

In other words, the 22% figure was arrived at by featuring only their most interesting current products, as well as then modifying the figures to essentially say, "Revenue growth that we would like you to focus on is for our sexiest product, minus all of the bad stuff we didn't manage well."

Second, most of the quoted paragraph discusses the most technological aspects of their then product portfolio. Note the words: "digital", "network", "laser" and so on. These words are meant to convey that Xerox is a technology company and current with the dot.com era in which these results were delivered, and by which the investment community was judging them.

Next, note the use of flowery language, such as, "outstanding", "excellent", "strong" and "good". Quantities speak for themselves, especially when related to the strategies laid out by management. There is no need to qualify actually good results with superfluous language.

Finally, and crucially, what does any of this have to do with their actual revenue performance which saw total revenues shrink by 1.1%? Not only that, but the sale of products – even including the sexiest products – actually shrank by 3.8%. Sadly, Xerox's best-performing revenue category in 1999 was servicing their existing product line. A clearer story about their impending obsolescence could not be told.

Subtleties

Importantly, financial statements include other clues about behavior besides the quantitative effects vs. qualitative behaviors story. How each account is described is also indicative of the underlying behavior of management. For example, one organization's bland net revenues, as compared to another's net sales to customers tells you a lot about the management of the two organizations and how they view customers. There is no reason to have a preference for one version over the other. These choices are expressions of the personalities that created the categories. In the second case, you can bet that internal discussions among management focus on customers, and not on revenues. This is even more interesting if management repeatedly emphasizes in its public comments how important they consider customers to be.

One organization's bringing forth of important data from the financial statement footnotes into its regular financial statement presentation, and then subsequent discussion of those nuanced but important details, is superior to the organization whose statements are more obscure. For example, key to understanding a manufacturing firm is the detail contained in the balance sheet's asset category: property, plant, and equipment. Most firms report one or three lines of information in the formal financial statements.

The one-line version reads, "Property, plant, and equipment, net." While the three-line version typically reports, "Property, plant, and equipment," followed by, "Depreciation and amortization," and concluding with, "Property, plant, and equipment, net." This is scarcely enough information to do a thorough analysis of critical information like calculating the average expected life of fixed assets, fraction of expected life exhausted, and average remaining years for the firm's most important assets. Furthermore, these calculations turn out to be critical to understand for the fundamental analyst trying to calculate maintenance capital expenditures for a free-cash flow analysis, and eventual valuation.

Yes, many firms put information in their footnotes to calculate these figures. But if a firm instead places the detailed data front-and-center in the formal balance sheet, it means that they know investors need to understand this information. Not only that, but it also means they consider the investment community's understanding as key to their success. All of this is, of course, good ABCDE. Imagine the breath of fresh air that occurs, only rarely, when a firm provides the following level of detail about property, plant, and equipment in prime-time (i.e., not buried in a footnote) as opposed to the more typical and obscure property and equipment, net.

- Land

- Buildings and improvements

- Machinery and equipment

- Computer hardware and software

- Leasehold improvements

- Construction in progress

- Capital leases – machinery and equipment

- Total property and equipment, gross

- Accumulated depreciation and amortization

- Property and equipment, net

A competitive advantage employed by Jason in his career has been to create individual quarterly statements for each company he examines. He does this because each of the major statements – the income statement, balance sheet, and cash flow statement – are reported on a different temporal basis. This makes evaluation of quarterly performance more difficult and time consuming for active investment managers.

So, imagine Jason's delight at discovering an organization, Quanta Services, that reported each of its financial statements on a quarterly basis. The company clearly wanted its shareholders to understand its quarterly performance, and thus took the extra step of doing this for its investors.

In summary for this section on behavioral financial statement analysis, everything a business does is evidence about the business. We prefer businesses that manage their ABCDE for the benefit of investors because we believe this leads to better performance for their securities, too.

Valuation as an indication of values

Valuation has the air of being quantitative, data-driven, and beyond human-interference, when in fact this is not true. Since the buying and selling of securities takes place in financial markets, and since we have demonstrated that financial markets are largely not discounting/ assessing fundamental measures and are driven by a very small percentage of investors on any given day, it makes sense to be more comprehensive in your approach if you want to capture the behavioral effects in a valuation.

Most valuation models consider behavior ham-handedly, in our opinion. They typically output something along the lines of: the fair value of a share of the XYZ Company, Inc. is $73.24. A common wrinkle added to valuation models in an attempt to make them more descriptive of the behavioral forces exhibited by financial markets is to have a best or high case, a median case, and a worst or low case. And still another wrinkle is to build a margin of safety into the fundamental valuation model that is arbitrary (e.g. 15%) or is based on some statistical measure like purchasing shares only when they are trading at least one standard deviation below the average price over some suggested period.

All of these are fine ideas in our opinion, but there are many other ways to build behavior into valuation models. Like what? For starters, since different investors utilize different factors to determine their buys and sells, it makes sense to factor these into your valuation. That is, some investors buy based on price-to-earnings ratios and their estimate of earnings per share for some future period. While others prefer price-to-EBITDA ratios as the basis for valuation. And still others like discounted cash flow, or free-cash-flow estimations of value.

In academic literature the focus is on discovering which of many popular valuation measures is most predictive of future securities returns, but this seems a spurious conversation. Why not calculate multiple valuations to gain better insight into the minds in the market? Since many fundamental analyses take as their raw inputs some form of projection of future business outcomes, like income statements, balance sheets, and cash flow statements, and since many fundamental valuation models are driven by these variables, then it is very simple to create multiple valuations.

You could build into a single aggregate fair value price estimate, the valuation based on price-to-revenues, price-to-operating income, price-to-EBITDA, price-to-earnings, price-to-total assets, price-to-book value, price-to-operating cash flow, price-to-free cash flow, and so forth. By gaining transparency into the likely assumptions of multiple investors – who are variously using each of these methods – and their opinion of the company, we believe a more accurate estimate of fundamental value is likely.[50]

Furthermore, any wild variations in the valuations can serve two valuable purposes. First, though it does not relate to a behavioral cue, it is a check on any mis-estimated figures in your valuation. If, for example, the price per share indicated by price-to-EBIT is significantly different from your valuation based on price-to-EBITDA, then it is a strong indication you have an error in your estimate of depreciation and amortization. Likewise, a big difference in valuation between price-to-sales and price-to-EBIT suggests something in your assumptions for operating expenses is off. This is an important check on the quality of your own work.

Second, actual insight into the minds of other market participants can be had. If, for example, your fundamental analysis suggests that investors who prefer price-to-book value paid a different price then those that utilize PE ratios, over time, then that is an insight into

---

[50]   This idea is not unique to us, and is put forth in James H. Zukin and John G. Mavredakis, *Financial Valuation: Businesses and Business Interests* (Warren, Gorham, and Lamont, 1 January 1990).

the behavior of the company's investors, who in turn determine the share price. Critical to this kind of work is evaluating the investment philosophies/strategies of the major stockholders over time. Hint: in the United States, the major stockholders each quarter report their holdings on a Form 4.

For example, if there was a time when a company had mostly a value contingent among its major shareholders, then an analysis of traditional value investor metrics like price-to-book value and discounted free cash flow reveals what the value crowd thought of the business. Likewise, if the major holders were mostly growth-oriented investors then measures often associated with that contingent like price-to-sales, price-to-earnings, and price-to-EBITDA may yield behavioral insights. Now, when valuing the business you can build into your model the possible behavior of investors because you can emphasize some valuation measures more than others depending on your view of what kind of investors are invested at that moment.

Another refinement to typical valuation models is to calculate for each business under consideration a high price, low price, and median price based on historical data. These prices then can be used to calculate historically high, median, and low multiples for the different measures (e.g. price-to-revenues through price-to-free cash flow). It is our experience that financial markets typically are consistent and persistent in ascribing multiples during different moments in the performance of a business over time. Said another way, when things are going well financial markets typically pay the same, or very similar, maximum multiples for a share in a business, and when things are going poorly they pay the same, or very similar, minimum multiples for a share. In this way, research analysts can build the various moods/behaviors of financial markets into their valuation models explicitly.

Table 4.6 shows data from Newell Brands (ticker: NWL) and the multiples paid for it by the market over many years.

Table 4.6: Newell Brands multiples over a period of five years

Multiple	Year 1	Year 2	Year 3	Year 4	Year 5	Avg.	Std. Dev.	CV
High P/E	14.65	13.83	12.55	10.42	10.14	12.32	2.01	16.0%
Avg. P/E	12.42	12.00	11.41	8.33	9.22	10.67	1.80	17.0%
Low P/E	9.15	10.36	10.38	7.01	8.16	9.01	1.45	16.0%
High P/EBIT	4.81	4.84	4.81	5.07	3.61	4.63	0.58	13.0%
Avg. P/EBIT	4.08	4.20	4.37	4.05	3.28	4.00	0.42	10.0%
Low P/EBIT	3.01	3.63	3.97	3.41	2.90	3.38	0.44	13.0%
High P/EBITDA	2.27	2.48	2.58	2.84	2.11	2.46	0.28	12.0%
Avg. P/EBITDA	1.93	2.15	2.35	2.27	1.91	2.12	0.20	9.0%
Low P/EBITDA	1.42	1.86	2.13	1.91	1.69	1.80	0.27	15.0%
High P/BV	1.12	1.39	1.41	1.49	1.21	1.32	0.15	12.0%
Avg. P/BV	0.95	1.20	1.28	1.19	1.10	1.15	0.13	11.0%
Low P/BV	0.70	1.04	1.17	1.00	0.98	0.98	0.17	18.0%
High P/assets	0.23	0.28	0.31	0.35	0.27	0.29	0.04	16.0%
Avg. P/assets	0.19	0.24	0.28	0.28	0.25	0.25	0.04	14.0%
Low P/assets	0.14	0.21	0.25	0.23	0.22	0.21	0.04	20.0%
High P/sales	1.87	2.16	2.29	2.58	1.91	2.16	0.29	13.0%
Avg. P/sales	1.59	1.87	2.08	2.06	1.74	1.87	0.21	11.0%
Low P/sales	1.17	1.62	1.89	1.73	1.54	1.59	0.27	17.0%
EPS	$0.47	$0.62	$0.75	$1.00	$0.87	$0.74	$0.21	28.4%

The table shows several things of importance. First, some of the most popular ways of valuing businesses used by investors, including: price to earnings (P/E); price to earnings before interest expense and taxes (P/EBIT); price to earnings before interest expense and taxes with depreciation and amortization added back (P/EBITDA); price to the net worth, or book value of the business (P/BV); price to total assets

(P/assets); and price to a firm's revenues, or sales (P/Sales). For each of these different and popular ways of valuing a business are shown the actual high, average, and low multiples paid during the course of a five-year period. In other words, the table provides transparency into the opinions of different constituencies of investors and how they valued Newell Brands over this time period.

For each of the rows, an average and standard deviation is calculated. The last column is of the most interest to us here, which shows the stability of the data as measured by the coefficient of variation (CV). Here is how it is calculated:

CV = standard deviation average

CV measures the extent of the volatility in data around its average. By comparing the CV for different, but related, data you can gain insight into investor behavior. For example, compare the above CV figures for the different valuation metrics to the diluted earnings per share CV of 28.4% over the same time frame. Said another way, the behavior of investors relative to this business is more consistent/less volatile (no CV greater than 28.4%) than the actual performance of the business as measured by its diluted earnings per share.

A conclusion that may be drawn from the data is that the shareholders that invest in Newell Brands are patient, since the consistency of their interest, as measured by the CV for the different valuation measures, is lower/less volatile than the company's actual operating performance. This normally would suggest that Newell has a cadre of value investors that make up the bulk of their investors. Also, the stability of each of the CVs calculated above and for the six different valuation measures demonstrates our point that investors are consistent in how they value a business.

Here is another way to use this kind of information. If the performance of the business has recently been above average, then it is reasonable to expect that the higher multiples are likely to prevail. Therefore, when valuing the business, you would want to use the higher multiples shown above to derive your estimates for value.

Or, do you anticipate a reversion to the mean based on economic headwinds that are sure to slow business performance down? If so, then you can revert to the mean, rather than high, valuation multiples paid for a business. The value derived is then more in line with your expectations.

As we discussed above, management's behaviors and character are captured in their company's financial statements. Therefore, it makes sense to take cues from financial statement analysis in estimating the future performance of the business in valuing it.

In the case of Xerox mentioned above, management said that they would deliver 10% top-line revenue growth for five years in the heart of the dot.com era. But, Jason's base-case model had them only growing revenues at 6% per year. This choice was made because of the quantitative and ABCDE-based evidence evaluated in the financial statements, as well as in the 'Management's Discussion and Analysis' section of the firm's annual report. Finally, the directly observed behavior of the investor relations professional with regard to one of its largest shareholders was the final straw (hint: get a dog-walker next time).

In-person analysis

In the preceding sections we emphasized an assessment of the behaviors embedded in financial results, yet active investment managers frequently have in-person interaction with the executive managers of securities in which they hold an interest. We are of course talking about earnings calls and one-on-one interviews with management. These are unparalleled moments during which clever active managers can really get a sense of the behavioral tendencies of management. These assessments then may be used to improve an understanding of the company.

Conference calls

While earnings season and its earnings calls are typically scripted and dull, they do also sometimes feature actionable intelligence. It is rare that the research analyst or portfolio manager can actually ask a question of management, because the sell-side analyst community is given the overwhelming majority of the questions. We are certain you have joined conference calls very early, pushed *1 as soon as you were joined in, and still your question is never reached. Nonetheless, management is exposing itself to scrutiny for around one hour each quarter and contained in those 60 minutes is evidence of management behavior, or ABCDE.

Below we discuss situations that we believe are strongly indicative of management behavior. Note: the indications are not necessarily good or bad, but they are indications of strong behavioral choices, and therefore worth the attention of research professionals. In particular, the following are important examples of behavioral cues on the part of management.

Candor

Be alert to press releases that do not directly describe business results, but which instead are published with much qualifying language and indirect answers to typical investor questions. Most obviously: How did the firm perform in its most recent quarter? It is entirely possible to answer questions simply and directly. Facts are usually explicit and also frequently self-evident. If management takes an entire paragraph or more to address a basic business issue that has a factual basis, this is noteworthy.[51]

Barricading

If management is spare in its financial results presentations – in either its press release or scripted sessions, especially relative to its competition – it is indicative of barricading. Remember that management has access to the innermost details of business performance and very likely on a daily business. Remember also that modern financial reporting technologies allow management to close the books within several days of a quarter's end. A lack of communication of these results is for a reason and usually a sign of bad ABCDE.

Management frequently argues that their financial results contain sensitive information that could be exploited by competition if they disclosed it in an earnings call. We are dubious of such claims. Execution of a solid business strategy on a daily basis by management is the source

---

[51] See for example the work of Rittenhouse Rankings, which evaluates executive candor, which the firm has turned into a quantitative measure. This measure is then used to construct an index that orders most candid firms to least candid firms, with the most candid handily, and consistently, beating the S&P 500.

of business competitive advantage, much more so than any intel let loose by publicly reporting financial results that are, on average, 45 days old. Instead, we believe that such obfuscation is evidence of bad management ABCDE.

Non-GAAP gap

Companies frequently craft non-Generally Accepted Accounting Principles (GAAP) performance measures that they tout in press releases and conference calls. To us, this frequently obscures direct understanding about specific data as much as it reveals. But from an ABCDE behavioral perspective it is always revealing.

Businesses create this gap in understanding, complaining that GAAP is too homogenous a reporting system to describe their supposedly heterogeneous world. However, the standards are generic on purpose so that just about every company and its uniqueness can be accurately described by its accounting. We consider it bad form for management to spend less than a majority of its in-person time with investors discussing GAAP measures when discussing quantitative results.

If management insists on emphasizing non-GAAP performance measures, it is an indication of their ABCDE and should raise questions for active investment managers. Questions like: Is management formally compensated based on these non-GAAP measures? Are these measures easily audited? How much judgment on the part of management is required in estimating these measures? Is the company on record with its official method for calculating these non GAAP-measures to ensure consistency and comparability over time? Or is management the only source for what numbers are used to calculate the alternative measures? If the company uses non-GAAP measures do they provide an explanation for how their preferred numbers are different from GAAP so that active investment managers may also estimate the numbers? Does the company's competition use similar measures to ensure comparability? If not, why not?

Q&A

Does management allow its actual investors and prospective investors (i.e., the buy-side) to ask questions on its conference calls, or is the Q&A the exclusive purview of the sell-side analyst community? If you never hear a fellow buy-side analyst on conference calls this is evidence of a management preference for influencing the sell-side analyst community. We say this fully understanding that many buy-side analysts and portfolio managers do not like to air their questions publicly for competitive reasons. Still, on occasion, buy-side questions ought to be a part of conference calls. But they rarely are.

Does management answer questions directly and succinctly per our points above regarding candor and barricading? Or do they avoid and/or obfuscate with an answer?

Are management comfortable answering questions with, "I don't know?" Management admitting its ignorance about something is certainly indicative of management behavior; in our experience, mostly good behavior.

How much hubris, if any, is on display by management in its relationship with the analyst community? Put simply, is there a customer first attitude, or chilly indifference?

Management's style

Listen to management and their choice of words in describing common business situations. Things like successes and failures and the word choice used to describe these things provide behavioral insights. Examples include: management downplaying its successes; downplaying the importance of quarterly earnings; emphasizing long-term strategy; discussing the importance of maintaining a par price on its bonds as more important than raising their stock price in times of trouble; and so forth. The preceding are examples of management humility and sobriety. This is in stark contrast to many management teams whose ABCDE is hubristic and grandiose.

One-on-ones

Each of the above points about conference calls is also valid in one-on-one interview settings. However, because of the interrogative and personal, private nature of one-on-one management conversations, there is a much greater ability to assess management behavior and character.

All of the techniques of successfully interviewing management to gain insight into management behavior rely on playing with contexts. This is because management teams are the primary source of information about their business, with all other sources being secondary, at best. Thus, management has heard just about every question there is about their businesses, and they are well-acquainted with all of the variations of the questions. Therefore, when you ask a direct question about a business, it gives management fundamental clues as to the context (i.e., it anchors them), and hence they know the correct answer for the context.

To glean information, active investment managers need to recognize the priming and anchoring effects (i.e., the unconscious contextualization) of their questions. Once research pros recognize their own contexts, as well as those of management, they can then play with the contexts so as to not prime/anchor management. Ideal question contexts are unfamiliar, yet tangent to the answer contexts. In other words, if you want to win a game of poker you must not show your hand. Not only that, but you must also become a master at controlling the information exchange between questioner and answerer.

An illustration of this technique from Jason's portfolio management career may prove useful. The example regards Devon Energy, and at a time when the fund family for whom Jason worked was the company's largest shareholder.

In-depth example of controlling context

It is 1999. Devon Energy (ticker symbol: DVN) is one of the largest independent oil and natural gas producers in the United States. They are renowned for their ability to make excellent acquisitions to grow their oil and natural gas reserves. They are also well known for their unusual production of natural gas from coal bed methane deposits. Typically, natural gas wells are very expensive to drill because natural gas is found deep in the earth. The weight of all that rock over the hydrocarbons causes them to turn into natural gas. So, a natural gas well might be drilled over 12,000 feet into the earth, whereas an oil well might be less than 1,000 feet. That's why Devon's coal bed methane technology is important. This gas is found as bubbles in water inhabiting coal seam deposits. And these coal deposits may only be 100 to 200 feet below the surface of the earth. This is a significantly cheaper well to dig, so the potential for economic returns is higher. The trick is extracting the natural gas from the bubbles. This is Devon's specialty.

Jason is in Denver for the Rocky Mountain Natural Gas Investment Forum. Devon publicly says its future cost of extraction will be much lower because of their huge coal bed methane properties in central Wyoming (near Gillette). This is a huge competitive advantage. Because there are coal bed methane deposits throughout the world, every research analyst and portfolio manager wants to know where Devon will invest next. Over the course of the day Jason watches countless numbers of folks ask a variation of this same question, "Where else are you looking?" But Devon doesn't want folks to know where they are looking. Any leak of their interest is valuable information for any competitor. Understandably, Devon's management has developed quite an intellectual fortress around this information.

All of this background information is needed so that you can understand the context of the one-on-one access. It is also needed because you can clearly see that if your question is of Type A – "Where else are you looking?" – and about Context A – "other coal bed methane properties" – then you get Answer A, or no useful answer at all – the intellectual fortress. Instead, active investment managers looking to examine managements' ABCDE need to alter the contexts of their questions if they hope to gain actionable and potentially valuable information. Remember, question contexts are ideally tangent, but unfamiliar to the answer context.

Here are some of the facts that went into Jason's construction of new question contexts.

First of all, Devon has a large number of executives at this smallish conference. This is unusual. During most conferences, only the upper management attends and each of them is very skilled at playing matador with an analyst's bull question. Jason's first essential observation is that potentially non-savvy executives are participating in the conference.

Jason therefore decides to focus on Devon's executive in charge of worldwide exploration because he is in charge of the information he wants to know and because he is potentially un-savvy. Jason begins by sitting on the periphery of the group of questioners surrounding the Devon exec. The question, "where else are you looking?" is asked in every possible permutation over the course of an hour and a half. No one gets the goods.

Jason is waiting for the right moment to spring his question context on the executive, when he notices that the tone of the conversation relaxes as the question context changes. At this particular moment the exec only has two sell-side analysts around him. They are discussing social, not business, things: "How are the wife and kids?" and "How's your [golf] handicap?"

First of all, note that Jason has chosen an executive who is one-step removed from the normal investment conference context, the person in charge of worldwide exploration, rather than someone from the C-suite. Next, also notice that the question context has shifted completely away from tangency relative to the answer context. Namely, the question and answer contexts have shifted by one degree from business to personal. In other words, people are more open and vulnerable now.

Jason, who knows that he looks very young for his age takes advantage of any representativeness bias (stereotype) that these men might have about a young investment professional. He is hoping that the air of someone young, ignorant, and naïve will lead to unguarded access to the answer context from his preferred question context.

Jason is a wolf in sheep's clothing and walks up to the three men who each acknowledge him.

Jason was sensitive to whether or not his strategy would work at this juncture, for around his neck was a name tag identifying him as a portfolio manager for the Davis Funds, Devon's largest shareholder. That none of the three men acknowledged the importance of the Davis Funds relative to Devon, Jason took as a sign that they had discounted him due to his youthful appearance, and that the question context had surely shifted to a non-business one.

When there was a break, Jason asked deferentially, "So this coal bed methane thing sounds like a home run, yes?" The two sell-side analysts laugh heartily at Jason's naïveté as the Devon exec answers the question.

That the group laughs at Jason's question means that the wall around the answer context is unmanned, and that there is an opportunity for the questioning strategy to work.

Devon's exec then goes on to explain to Jason all about their coal bed methane prospects. All the while Jason nods back at the exec as if he is delivering new revelations to this neophyte investor. Jason then asks another naïve question that he already knows the answer to: "Where in the world are coal bed methane deposits?"

Before Devon's exec has the chance to answer, the two sell-siders enjoy another condescending moment at Jason's (supposed) expense, and say almost in unison, "Everyone knows that. They are in lots of places, like the former Soviet Union, Czech Republic, Poland, Canada, Kazakhstan ..."

At that moment when Jason detects Devon's exec is vulnerable he goes in for the kill with an unusual, though tangent question context, speaking through the verbal cacophony of the two sell-side pomps, he asks: "And what foreign languages are you studying?"

Devon's exec replies without recognizing that the question context is tangent to the answer context: "Czech and Pol ... i ... sh." Jason says, "Thank you," and walks away with his alpha-earning treasure.

Again, for this kind of situation to work requires the question context to be tangent to the answer context. Why? It may seem as if Jason could have asked his context-break question at the very beginning, but consider the position of most people asked a context-less question, such as, "What foreign languages are you studying?" A question whose context is so far afield from the context of a conversation is likely to raise an interviewee's defenses. Consequently, tangency of a question context is essential for the above behavioral detection technique to work.

Jason also had to reestablish the business context with his questions about coal bed methane. Crucially though, he chose an air of naïveté that left the executive and the sell-side analysts around him vulnerable. They remained rooted in their context – comfortable conversation about their personal lives – while indulging Jason's interruption. Had Jason been more serious in his approach and demeanor it is likely that the Devon executive would not have remained vulnerable.

Now it might have been the case that Jason's Devon strategy would not have worked. In fact, there are examples from Jason's career in which this strategy did not work. However, they were rare. Also, while altering contexts may fail occasionally, the traditional method of matching question contexts to answer contexts is always available, and with their almost universal bland, non-alpha generating information.

There are other ways of altering contexts in order to glean alpha-generating information in a one-on-one interview. For example, you can present your beliefs about a company in an exaggerated way to see if management goes out of its way to downplay, or to correct, your beliefs.

Dissecting this technique, you can see that you take the standard answer context – that is, the Wall Street consensus – and force it to be unusual, but tangent to the typical view of a company.

For example, when most analysts feel a company is a buy and not a strong buy, you could state: "My model seems to suggest your firm is undervalued by 30%, or more." You then examine to see if management goes out of its way to re-establish the standard context, something such as, "No, no, that's too aggressive." Whether they try and re-establish the standard context or not, their response is telling.

It could be that the business re-establishing the consensus context is evidence that management wants to under-promise and over-deliver on its performance, in recognition of the strong behavioral response to performance disappointments on the part of investors. In this instance, the response is indicative of a management that is managing its investors (bad ABCDE).

Management could also push you back to the consensus view because they actually care that you succeed as an investor in their company (good ABCDE). In other words, they are trying to navigate you back to the truth. Here, the active investment manager gains insight into the likely performance of the business, which is obviously important information. By asking other questions that establish the motivations of management – are they managing their investors or actually being helpful? – assists tremendously in ascertaining which of the two preceding scenarios is taking place.

What if management does not try and move you back to the consensus question context? Again, there are two possibilities. The first possibility is that management does not see it as valuable to correct the contexts that surround its business. Hopefully it is clear that this also may be a good thing, or a bad thing. If they do not care about the investor contexts regarding their business it could be that they are primarily focused on executing their strategy for the long term, recognizing that owners of shares are likely high-turnover, non-vested in business success, speculators. On the other hand, it could be that they are just insensitive to this particular management nuance.

Second among the possibilities if management does not correct your exaggerated view of their future performance is that you are correct. Once again, this is an extremely beneficial edge that increases the probability that you have gained an alpha-edge in your analytical work.

The ability to alter question contexts regardless of the form takes time to develop. Skills here are reliant on a combination of knowledge, intelligence, creativity, and intuition. Nonetheless, wise and intelligent contextualization is an advantage available to active investment managers, and that eludes that of passive investors, or those not taking advantage of in-person conversations.

Lie and truth detection

An additional marquee benefit of one-on-one interviews is the ability to tell whether or not management of a business is telling you the truth or lying to you. When discussing this skill most investors find the ability to detect lies more appealing than the ability to detect the truth. This preference for lie detection over truth detection is likely evidence of loss aversion at work. Most of us hate to be lied to more than we appreciate being told the truth, because each of us has experienced the outsized pain of loss from being the victim of a lie.

However, just as there are Type I and Type II errors in statistics, the same is true in interviewing management. Said plainly, it is certainly an error in judgment to purchase a security in a company that is lying to you about an important piece of data. But it is also an error to sell a security in a company because you believe they are lying to you, when in fact they are not. Keep this in mind as we tread into the subject of lie/truth detection.

Jason, in conjunction with globally respected lie detection experts, conducted history's first research into the ability of research analysts and portfolio managers to detect lies,[52],[53] both within finance and investing, and in our personal lives. In short, we investment pros are terrible at it.

A meta-analysis of the evidence found that globally people are about 54% able to make correct lie-truth judgments.[54] This score is based on

---

[52] Maria Hartwig, Jason A. Voss and D. Brian Wallace, 'Detecting Lies in the Financial Industry: A Survey of Investment Professionals' Beliefs', *Journal of Behavioral Finance* 16:2 (2015), pp. 173–182.

[53] Maria Hartwig, Jason A. Voss, Laure Brimbal and D. Brian Wallace, 'Investment Professionals' Ability to Detect Deception: Accuracy, Bias and Metacognitive Realism', *Journal of Behavioral Finance* 18:1 (2017), pp. 1–13.

[54] Charles F. Bond, Jr. and Bella M. DePaulo, 'Accuracy of Deception

a study of studies (i.e., a meta-analysis) that aggregated the results of 206 lie-truth judgment research papers featuring over 24,000 subjects. In these studies a ground truth is known by the scientists, and so they are able to measure accurately people's ability to discern lies and truth. The 54% score can be further broken down into its component parts with people, globally, on average being able to correctly classify 47% of lies as deceptive, and 61% of truths as non-deceptive.

The score of 54% may seem a high percentage, but it is just slightly better than a 50:50 guess about whether people are hearing a lie, or hearing the truth. In research conducted by Jason, financial professionals are actually worse than the general public at lie-truth judgments, logging just a 49.4% accuracy for all types of lies, and within financial settings it is only slightly better at 51.8%.[55] Note: this is still below average, relative to that found among all people globally.

There are many reasons for this poor lie detection performance, but one is that most people, including research professionals, believe the pan-cultural myth that lies are revealed/leaked by body language cues called micro-expressions and that these are the key to detecting lies. This has been demonstrated as a false assumption in dozens upon dozens of studies dating back to at least 1958. Definitively stated, body language and micro-expressions are poor indicators of lies or truth being communicated.

The theory of body language cues as indicative of lies rests on some poor assumptions. Primary among the assumptions is that liars are

---

Judgments', *Personality and Social Psychology Review* 10:3 (2006), pp. 214–234.
[55]   Maria Hartwig, Jason A. Voss, Laure Brimbal and D. Brian Wallace, 'Investment Professionals' Ability to Detect Deception: Accuracy, Bias and Metacognitive Realism', *Journal of Behavioral Finance* 18:1 (2017), pp. 1–13.

more anxious than truth-tellers in situations where the stakes are important. This anxiety is believed to be leaked out via body language. Consequently, a commonly-taught law enforcement interview technique seeks to increase the anxiety level in interrogative questioning.

But this assumption overlooks the fact that both liars and truth-tellers have reasons to be anxious in a situation where the stakes are important. Liars may be anxious because they fear discovery. However, truth-tellers may be anxious because they fear being falsely accused of something. So, even if micro-expressions are indicative of an underlying behavior such as interviewee anxiety, it is not necessarily an indication that they are lying.

Another faulty assumption of the body-language, micro-expression community is that these very subtle expressions are noticeable at all. In study after study, researchers are unable to replicate results from the sole researcher claiming that micro-expressions are indicative of lies.[56]

Continuing on, another reason that most people fail to detect lies is that most of us are very good liars. We do not state the following glibly, but it is true for most people that starting at a very young age we are encouraged to lie, especially in social situations. Most of us were admonished, for instance, by our parents to say one thing, while we felt or believed another. These lies are done for the sake of social niceties. Can you really say that your spouse does not look good in their chosen attire for the evening out at the party?

---

[56] For a review of this literature, see Maria Hartwig and Jason A. Voss, 'Lie Detection Guide: Theory and Practice for Investment Professionals', CFA Institute (January 2017).

If body language does not work, what does?

There are two things that have been demonstrated empirically to work. One is text-based analysis using the data reported by the software, Linguistic Inquiry and Word Count (LIWC, pronounced, 'luke'), and, second, Strategic Use of Evidence (SUE). While a full discussion of these techniques is not our focus here, the point is that examining management's ABCDE, specifically separating out lies from truth, is possible and frequently valuable.

Briefly, LIWC evaluates text-based communications for many different behavioral criteria. Behind the scenes of the software, a group of human linguistic experts routinely gather to evaluate the meaning of words, and common ways of communicating ideas and emotions, which drift over time. For example, the word 'sick' previously meant someone whose physical or mental health was poor. However, it now can mean in urban environments something that is edgy and desirable, such as, "those sneakers are sick!" LIWC is not specifically designed to catch lies, though some of its criterion consider lying-like behaviors, such as 'Authentic,' and 'Tentativeness.' LIWC also reports on many other management ABCDE that may prove useful to your analyses. Examples include: amount of positive and negative emotive words; levels of anxiety, sadness, certainty; and the amount of past versus future orientation.

SUE as a questioning technique flips traditional interrogative lie-detection interviewing on its head. Traditionally those looking to separate lies from truth were instructed to present evidence (though not proof) of suspicious behavior immediately in order to shock an interviewee. Thus, having supposedly creating anxiety, interviewers were then to look for the micro-expressions believed indicative of lies.

Sadly, this technique is a miserable way to detect lies. Why? Because you essentially tell every interviewee what evidence they need to explain logically in order for you to believe them. This is a poor use of evidence.

SUE works because its theory is actually descriptive of human behavior. Yes, both liars and truth-tellers have a reason to be anxious in an interview situation. Yes, both parties also want the interviewer to believe they are telling the truth. However, liars and truth-tellers have different strategies for convincing interviewers of the veracity of their words. When liars believe a questioner is close to knowing that they are lying, they become evasive and try to direct the conversation away from the evidence. Whereas truth-tellers' strategy is to directly guide questioners to important evidence so that they are exonerated or proven right.

Put another way, the next time you are interviewing management and you suspect, but cannot prove, they are lying, do not present your evidence by asking them directly to explain it. Instead, gradually narrow down the context surrounding your evidence and note the behavior of management: are they evasive or direct in answering your questions?

As an example, imagine you have evidence about a WiFi router manufacturer's sales in their overwhelmingly most important market, Southeast Asia. Your evidence – based on your own inventory channel checks – suggests that the sales are not as strong as management projected for the quarter. Also imagine that management has yet to revise expectations for quarterly earnings downward. Here you have evidence of a lack of forthrightness, though not necessarily a lie. Also, you know that channel checks are, at best, a sampling technique. What if your sample was bad? If you sell shares in the company and it turns out that you were wrong then you may miss out on share gains. This is a perfect time and place for SUE.

An initial question in an interview with the company might be, "How was the quarter?" This gives an executive her first opportunity to direct you to the negative performance of the WiFi routers in Southeast Asia which is the behavior of a truth-teller. Though realistically it is probably still too early in the line of questioning and too broad a question for them to specifically address the Southeast Asian router performance. But, imagine if the answer to your question about the quality of the quarter's performance is: "It was great!" It may have been that, but as you close in on your evidence that router sales were poor in Southeast Asia it makes it harder to walk back from an initial positive answer that the quarter was great.

Your follow up question could be, "What about the performance of the QXZ routers?" Here you have narrowed the context down slightly, but you still have not revealed your evidence about the independent channel checks. Here the honest executive is given another opportunity to take you to the evidence and to explain the performance. They may say at this juncture, "Southeast Asia underperformed, but the rest of our regions performed well."

Importantly, because they do not know about your evidence, they may not know you want them to address the possible poor performance of routers in Southeast Asia. In the aggregate, it could still be the case that their answer, an honest one, is, "QXZ routers sold well globally." By contrast, a lying executive may, at this point, be a bit evasive about his answer. He might say, "Printers sold great." This would of course be evading the question. If the executive – either liar or truth-teller – answers your question with, "They sold well," then you need to again narrow the context. But, again, note that their answer backs them slowly into a corner. These first two answers, "The quarter was great," and, "QXZ routers sold well" make it very difficult for them to walk the story back to the truth if they are, in fact, lying. Also, remember they still do not know about your independent channel checks.

Your next question might be, "How was performance in Southeast Asia?" Here you do not mention the QXZ router, just the region. Again, note the executive's willingness to provide direct evidence, or instead a desire to evade the line of questioning. At this point, the executive is likely to see that you are narrowing in on your ultimate question about the sale of the QXZ router in Southeast Asia. An honest executive is very likely to guide you to the information, something like, "That router so far has not sold so well in the quarter. We may guide down for the quarter." Whereas, a less reputable executive may start to tell you about the printer business, or try and change the subject, or they may ask you a question in return, "You've never asked this level of detail before, why now?" Evasiveness in the presence of a narrowing question context is very frequently indicative of deceitful behavior.

There are many additional details that make a trained SUE professional a highly-skilled lie detector, but they are outside the scope of our book.

Chapter review and what is to come

We reviewed multiple sources of information about behavior in this chapter on fundamental analysis. Added to your fundamental analysis repertoire should be the skills of:

- Viewing the financial statements as evidence of management actions/behaviors/choices/decisions/ethics (ABCDE).

- Incorporating the behavior of financial markets and of management explicitly into your valuation model to better estimate fair value securities pricing.

- Listening to company conference calls for important evidence about management behavior.

- Taking advantage of intelligent and wise contextualization in your one-on-one encounters with the executive management teams of businesses.

- Two techniques, LIWC and SUE, for improving your lie-truth judgments.

In *ROAM*'s next chapter we discuss how to conduct a manager search to identify high-quality active investment managers.

Chapter 5.
Prescriptions for Manager Search

A performance puzzle

B RUCE BENNETT WAS working as a consultant for a large investment platform, to identify successful investment managers for clients. Frequently they came with an idea in mind about what kind of investment manager they want, "We need a new mid-cap core manager, our current one is underperforming."

A computer evaluation tool had been designed to surface quality investment managers from many who manage money in accord with the style clients prefer. Bruce has entered updated data from many investment managers into the spreadsheet model and it has spit out about two dozen candidates.

Frankly, Bruce is confused. He knows from experience that there is a renowned investment manager for this style that was not showing up in the manager search. Rather than accept the managers surfaced by the model, he decided to manually enter the data of the manager he had heard to be high-quality to see its dossier relative to the competition.

Digging to the bottom

When looking at a 40-quarter return plot of the presumed high-quality investment manager, he saw that the investment manager had handily beaten its benchmark in 37 of the quarters, and that in the three quarters of underperformance the manager had barely underperformed. 'Hmmm,' thought Bruce, 'he is indeed a top manager!'

The reason the manager scored so poorly against his peers was that the values for risk, standard deviation in the Sharpe ratio, and beta in the Treynor ratio, were gigantic relative to the manager's peers. "How can this be? The outperformance was steady for ten years and *large*."

Much to Bruce's surprise, he discovered that these measures were not really measures of the chance of loss, which the rest of the world believes is the definition of risk. Instead, these measures evaluate the fluctuations around an average (in the case of standard deviation), and a sloped line (in the case of beta). In other words, the measures were registering the outperformance of the high-quality investment manager as *risk*. When, in fact, this is exactly the manager you want: one with upside volatility, but minimal downside volatility, relative to an investment benchmark.

Bruce was bothered by this inconsistency and wondered what other problems he would uncover with how the industry goes about identifying superior fund managers.

The past performance conundrum

The goal of active management is to generate returns for the investor that exceed the returns earned by simply and cheaply investing in an index fund. It seems logical to pick funds that have achieved this goal in the past. Virtually everyone, both professionals and individuals, rely heavily on past performance when deciding upon funds in which to invest.

The problem is that past performance is a very noisy, often misleading, predictor of future performance. Every investment product is required to disclose exactly this: *Past performance is not indicative of future performance*. Reams of academic research confirm this to be the case.

But despite this overwhelming evidence, past performance is the primary criteria used for picking funds. This is an example of the representativeness bias, where decisions are made based on characteristics that have little or no predictive power, but are emotionally appealing. And this bias is nowhere stronger than it is in investment markets.

The lack of predictive power is the consequence of two drivers, one an industry structure and the other the nature of investment returns.

First, is the powerful closet indexing factory, an outgrowth of industry incentives. Wishing to grow AUM, funds respond slavishly to the MPT-based emotional catering tools of minimizing volatility, tracking error, and style drift. A small fund with good performance wishing to grow is strongly incented to submit to these performance criteria, thus turning themselves into a closet indexer and underperforming, because you cannot beat the benchmark if you are the benchmark. In this way, poor performance follows superior performance as night follows the day (well not quite this predictable but awfully close). Past performance thus does not predict future performance.[57]

---

[57] A rational, theoretical explanation for the existence of the closet indexing factory is provided by Jonathan Berk and R. C. Green, 'Mutual Fund Flows and Performance in Rational Markets', *Journal of Political Economy* 112:6 (2004), pp. 1269–1295. They argue that it is rational for funds to capture the rents of

Second, is the statistical nature of investment returns. Hendrik Bessembinder finds that the reason the average stock generates a positive return is due to the positive skewness of returns.[58] The median monthly stock return is near zero, but the size of positive returns exceeds the absolute size of negative returns so the average stock return is positive. Bessembinder is one of the first researchers to isolate the critical importance of positive skewness for investment performance.

It is the case that fund performance relative to its benchmark displays positive skewness as well. A study by Paul Kaplan and Maciej Kowara dramatically demonstrates this.[59] Based on a worldwide sample of 5,500 active equity mutual funds, they find two-thirds outperform their benchmarks, gross of fees, over the 15-year period of 2003 through 2017.[60] But the most surprising (disturbing?) result was that the typical *outperforming* fund actually *underperformed* for a period of 9–12 years within this 15-year sample period. This means that the outperformance takes place in only three to six years out of a 15-year holding period.[61]

They found mirror results for the typical fund that underperformed during this 15-year time period: it outperformed for a period of 9–12 years. They conclude that three-, five-, and ten-year performance are very unreliable predictors of a fund's long-term performance and

---

their stock picking skill by growing large, thus earning higher fees, but, in turn, generating lower returns for their investors.

[58]   Hendrik Bessembinder, 'Do Stocks Outperform Treasury Bills?', *Journal of Financial Economics* 129:3 (2018), pp. 440–457.

[59]   Paul D. Kaplan and Maciej Kowara, 'How Long Can a Good Fund Underperform Its Benchmark?', Morningstar Manager Research (2018).

[60]   Gross of fees is used rather than net of fees due to the wide variation in fees across countries.

[61]   This does not mean the typical outperforming fund underperforms 9 to 12 years out of the 15, but instead outperforms for 9 to 12 continuous year periods, during which there will be both under and out performing years.

should not be used.[62] The positive skewness that is so important for fund performance can be hidden for extended periods and the benefit of it can only be harvested with long holding periods.

No matter how you cut it, past performance is not a reliable predictor of future performance. So, what is? Before we address this question, let's explore the widely-held belief that active managers lack skill.

Active managers stink, don't they?

It is a well-known fact that active investment managers cannot beat the market, yes? We do not dispute this record. However, there is something very interesting lurking in the data that deserves your attention.

Multiple studies over the last 20 years have documented that many active equity managers are skilled and do indeed earn excess returns on their stock holdings.[63] Prominent among them, Randy Cohen, Christopher Polk, and Bernhard Silli find that ex-ante *best-idea stocks*, as measured by the highest relative weight within a portfolio, earn a 6% alpha.[64] Stock alpha declines monotonically with rank, as can be seen in Figure 5.1.

---

[62] The irony of a Morningstar study arguing against using three-, five-, ten-year performance for picking a fund should not be missed, as these returns are the basis of their widely used Star fund rating system.

[63] K. J. Martijn Cremers, Jon A. Fulkerson and Timothy B. Riley, 'Challenging the Conventional Wisdom on Active Management: A Review of the Past 20 Years of Academic Literature on Actively Managed Mutual Funds', Working Paper (2018).

[64] Randolph Cohen, R. B., C. Polk and B. Silli, 'Best ideas', Harvard Working Paper (2010).

Figure 5.1: Stock annual alpha by best idea rank

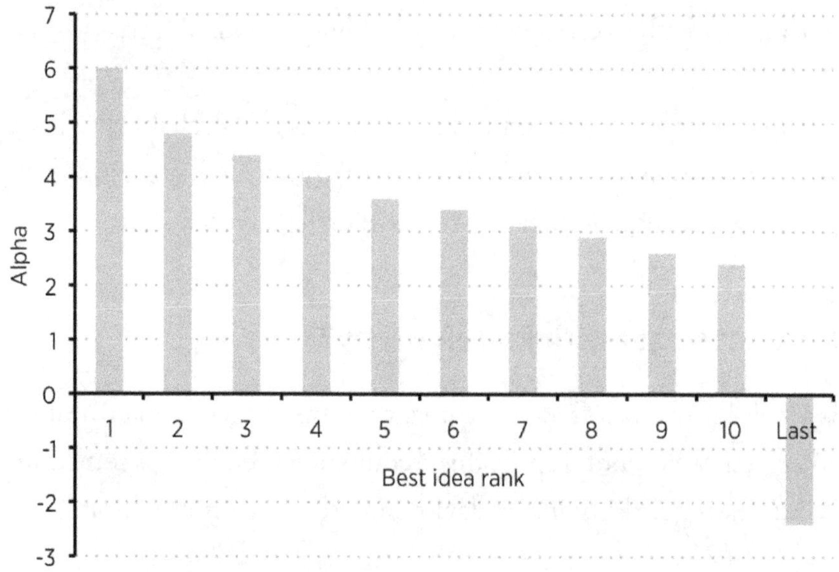

Based on Graph 3 in Randy Cohen, Christopher Polk, and Bernhard Silli (2010). Best Ideas, Harvard Business School working paper. Graph shows the average, over the subsequent quarter, six-factor risk adjusted annual alpha for the most overweighted stock in a mutual fund portfolio, the next most overweighed, and so forth. Based on all active US equity mutual funds from 1991 through 2005.

What this demonstrates quite clearly is that active equity mutual funds can identify best idea stocks and they can also ex-ante rank them in terms of future performance and overweight them accordingly.

The relative weight methodology of Cohen, Polk, and Silli can be used to rank the return potential of each stock held by an active equity mutual fund. The impact on a fund's portfolio return of investing in highly ranked stocks (i.e., high conviction stocks) is shown in Figure 5.2. If a fund commits an additional 10% to its top ten stocks, portfolio return improves by 61 basis points (bp). In turn, an additional 10% committed to the next ten highest ranked stocks bumps up portfolio return by 23 bp. However, if more is committed to stocks ranked lower than 20, fund returns decline, as indicated by the right most bar in Figure 5.2.

Figure 5.2: Fund annual return impact of 1% increase in stock ideas, by rank

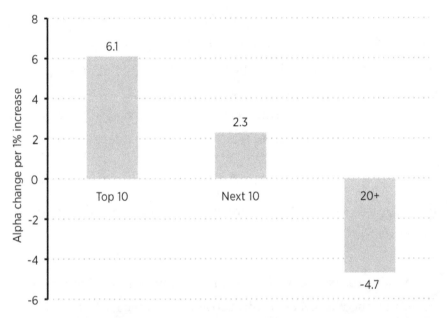

Based on single variable, subsequent gross fund alpha regressions estimated using a data set of 44m stock-month equity fund holdings over Jan 2001–Sep 2014. Data Source: Morningstar.

Figure 5.2 provides further evidence that investing in best-idea stocks generates higher fund returns. Practically, what this means is that any restriction imposed on a fund that mandates holding anything other than best-idea stocks negatively affects a fund's alpha. If enough mandates are added, a potential positive alpha is transformed into an actual negative alpha.

The fund distribution system is full of such restrictions. The net result is a fund distribution system that is a closet indexing factory, alpha-destroying juggernaut.

To be clear, we are talking about those who run the distribution system, both inside and outside the fund. The internal sales and marketing teams work hand in glove with the external platforms – broker-dealers, investment platform analysts, registered investment advisers (RIAs), and institutional investors – imposing value-destroying restrictions on investment teams. The returns generated by an analyst's investment decisions are eaten up by fund fees and the external restrictions placed on the fund.

This captures a primary concept with respect to fund investment management:

> Anything that restricts a fund's ability to invest in best ideas hurts performance. In other words, active equity managers should be free to *roam* about the equity universe in the consistent pursuit of their investment strategy.

This concept will pop up repeatedly throughout the remainder of this chapter.

Manager behavior is key

The evidence is clear: past performance is an unreliable predictor of future performance. But, as was hinted at in the previous section, manager behavior is predictive. The importance of fund manager behavior is not well known and is the focus of the following sections.

Strategy consistency

An important fund manager behavior is the consistent pursuit of a narrowly-defined strategy. The challenge is how to measure consistency. A common approach is to demand consistent returns over time. But we know that the best funds outperform at times and underperform at others. While this is emotionally difficult for investors, it is an unavoidable fact when investing in successful active funds. Strategies don't perform well in all types of markets.

Another distinction that is becoming blurred is that an index and a benchmark are the same thing. We both believe in evaluative standards and that the concept of benchmarking is a sound one. But using indices as benchmarks and then as strategies hurts active investment managers' potential to do the good work of earning alpha for their clients. To us, why not evaluate investment performance using customized benchmarks that are based on the stated investment universe of investment managers, along with the constraints dictated by their actual investment strategy?

Pioneering work by Ron Surz called Portfolio Opportunity Distributions (POD) takes this very approach. This performance- and risk-evaluation technique examines the strategy laid out by the investment manager in the prospectus and explores all possible portfolios the manager may have held within these constraints. It then compares actual manager performance to these opportunity sets.

This approach unshackles managers from being compared to an index. Instead, they are measured against their opportunity set, and their skill measured based on their ability to select investments from this set. What this does is liberate the manager to execute her strategy to the best of her ability. It also has the advantage of giving back to clients actual strategic alternatives for delivering total return, rather than just those dictated by the style box.

Similarity of holdings with fellow strategy investors

Another approach to gauge strategy consistency is to examine the type of stocks in which a manager invests. For example, is a value fund invested in value stocks, or is it chasing an unrelated trend such as favoring growth stocks?

Using a top-down process, Tom likes to evaluate the consistency of a manager by comparing their holdings to other managers pursuing the same strategy. He then creates a pool of stocks most held by these strategy managers.[65] For a manager following a *valuation* strategy, for example, the pool is comprised of stocks most held by other *valuation* funds.

It makes intuitive sense to use a screen driven by those who are looking for similar stock characteristics. It is worth noting that strategy pools are in constant motion, as managers make buy and sell decisions based on ever changing economic and market conditions. A stock stays in a strategy-pool for 14 months on average. Unlike the fixed size/value boxes of the style grid, this produces a dynamic process in which stocks of most interest to the manager are constantly changing. That is, the best results are obtained when the investment team moves about the equity universe in pursuit of own-strategy stocks.

---

[65] See C. Thomas Howard, 'The Importance of Investment Strategy', Working Paper (2010), for details on how strategy stock pools are created.

Figure 5.3: US active equity fund annual alpha by strategy consistency quartile

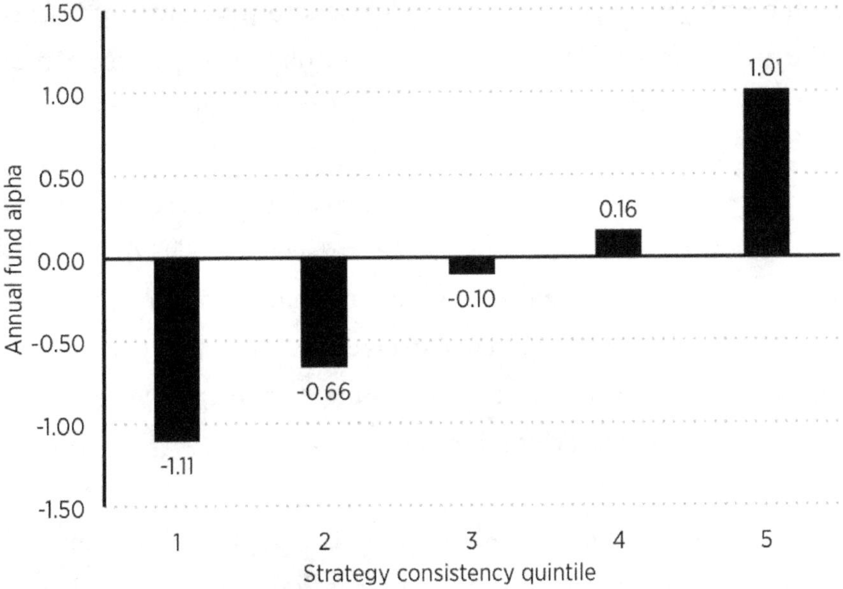

Strategy consistency is measured as the % of own strategy stocks held by the fund. Sample includes US Equity Funds from 1997–2017, resulting in 288,000 fund-month observations. Sources: Morningstar and AthenaInvest.

Focusing on similar strategy stocks is not only logically appealing but it leads to better fund performance. Figure 5.3 demonstrates that active equity funds holding the most similar strategy stocks (quintile 5 in Figure 5.3) outperform those holding the least similar strategy stocks by 212 basis points. This confirms the advantage of focusing on stocks most held by others following the same strategy. The collective intelligence of active equity fund managers provides valuable information for not only the best idea stocks, as demonstrated in Figures 5.1 and 5.2, but also identifies the most attractive pool of stocks upon which to focus.

Break out of the style box

We question the assumption that *style* refers to something of interest to the fund manager. When evaluating portfolio managers, the natural place to begin is their declaration about their investment strategy.

Next, there are several measures that were created to measure whether or not investment managers are toeing the lines of the style box. Here, of course, we are referring to style drift and tracking error. Both measures are not predictive of management success as measured by alpha. Instead, they are most indicative of the probability a manager has of a beta approaching 1.0, or is a closet indexer.

The strategy-consistency results reported in Figure 5.3 are in stark contrast to what has been uncovered regarding style-box consistency. Russ Wermers finds that equity funds experiencing the largest style drift outperform those with the least style drift by about 300 basis points.[66] Asking a fund manager to stay style-box consistent hurts performance because it forces them to invest in stocks outside their own strategy simply to track the style benchmark. Style box consistency begets strategy inconsistency and, in turn, hurts performance.

Ignore the style box. Instead, focus on the actual strategy of the investment manager and their likely ability to deliver alpha in execution of their approach. If you insist on elevating the style box in your manager searches, then at least abandon use of style drift and tracking error if you can verify that a manager's performance is best explained by careful application of their style.

---

[66] R. Wermers, 'A Matter of Style: The Causes and Consequences of Style Drift in Institutional Portfolios', University of Maryland Working Paper (2012).

High-conviction stocks

As was demonstrated earlier in this chapter, there is a performance advantage if a fund invests exclusively in high-conviction stocks. However, the typical mutual fund holds 75 stocks (the median number of holdings) and is thus badly over-diversified, investing in three times more alpha-destroying stocks than alpha-building stocks.

This provides further support for the argument that active equity funds should not grow too large (no larger than $1bn in AUM), nor be asked to minimize tracking error, style drift, and volatility – all of which encourage investing in non-high-conviction stocks.

Funds that consistently pursue a narrowly-defined strategy while taking high-conviction positions perform best. Past performance, if used at all, should play a secondary role in the fund selection process. Fund behavior, in terms of consistency and conviction, should be the focus.

Volatility ≠ risk

As we discussed earlier, volatility and risk are not the same thing. It is universally the case that risk is defined as the chance of loss. Volatility – either standard deviation or beta – does not measure just the chance of loss. Instead it is the weighted average of movements around an underlying average or the bumpiness of the ride.

This means that investment managers with strong outperformance relative to their benchmarks have more volatility than those that do not. This would not be a bad thing, except that when we take volatility as a proxy for the chance of loss then we create problems:

- We obscure the excellent outperformance on the part of some investment managers. Not only that, but these are actually the investment managers with the very strongest outperformance.

- Asset managers desire greater assets under management in order to take full advantage of their business models. Consequently, managers that understand that strong outperformance relative to a benchmark leads to too much volatility, and hence the mistaken appearance of risk, have a strong incentive to not outperform by much. In other words, there are strong incentives to act as a closet indexer rather than as a truly active manager.

This is not temporarily true. It will always be true if standard deviation or beta are used incorrectly as proxies for risk. If manager search professionals insist on using a measure of risk in evaluating the performance of an investment manager, then we strongly suggest they utilize concepts such as semi-standard deviation (i.e., Sortino ratio), or semi-beta as true measures of risk.

Manager search professionals should be striving to identify active investment managers with high upside performance and low downside performance. A simple ratio of positive semi-standard deviation to negative semi-standard deviation would be a shorthand way of identifying quality managers quickly. Alternatively, manager search professionals could simply calculate the skewness of investment managers and give preference to those with high positive skewness.

We suggest abandoning standard deviation and beta as measures of risk. However, beta remains useful as a measure of how closely a fund tracks its benchmark, but not as a measure of risk.

True individual stock risk

We want to emphasize that the true risk to investors for individual stocks is the suite of risks confronted by the company that issues them. If a research analyst or portfolio manager is confident that a company can generate enough revenues to cover its operating expenses, interest expense, capital investment needs, and to have monies left over, then the risk of a fluctuating security price is seen for what it truly is, evidence of the emotions of those trading the security.

As we argued in Chapter 1, most security price movements are not in response to fundamental changes in the performance of a business. Instead, the volatility is mostly due to irrational, or emotional reactions on the part of investors.

Ensure that active investment managers understand the true risks faced by the businesses or securities in which they invest.

Active equity opportunity

In recent years, many of the best funds, which we define as those that consistently pursue a narrowly-defined strategy while taking high-conviction positions, have underperformed. This begs the question of whether returns to stock picking vary over time. Indeed, there is considerable anecdotal evidence that stock picking is effective in certain market environments while not in others.

Academic research confirms this – with studies by Larry Gorman, Steven Sapra, and Robert Weigand; Antti Petajisto; and Anna von Reibnitz – providing a basis for measuring how favorable or unfavorable the current market environment is for stock picking.[67] They paint a picture in which the returns-to-skill rise in tandem with increased stock return cross-sectional dispersion and skewness, along with greater market volatility. That is, high levels of cross-sectional and longitudinal volatility represent a stock picker's nirvana.

Based on these articles, Tom created active equity opportunity (AEO), a measure of how active the emotional crowds are at a given time. The more active the crowds, the greater the returns-to-skill are and vice versa.

AEO is estimated as a scaled, weighted average of these four components, listed from most to least important:

1. Individual stock cross-sectional standard deviation.

2. Individual stock cross-sectional skewness.

3. CBOE Volatility Index (VIX).

4. Expected small stock premium.

The resulting monthly values for AEO from December 1998 through January 2019 are presented in Figure 5.4. The average AEO over this time-period is 40, which means values greater than 40 signal a better environment for stock picking while lower values signal a worse environment. During this 20-year time sample, 1998 through 2006 and 2008 through 2010 favored stock picking.

---

[67]   Larry Gorman, Steven Sapra and Robert Weigand, 'The Cross-Sectional Dispersion of Stock Returns, Alpha and the Information Ratio', *Journal of Investing* 19:3 (2010), pp. 113–127; Antti Petajisto, 'Active Share and Mutual Fund Performance' *Financial Analyst Journal* (2013); Anna von Reibnitz, 'When Opportunity Knocks: Cross-Sectional Return Dispersion and Active Fund Performance', *Critical Finance Review* 6:2 (2017), pp. 303–356.

Figure 5.4: Active equity opportunity (1997–2019)

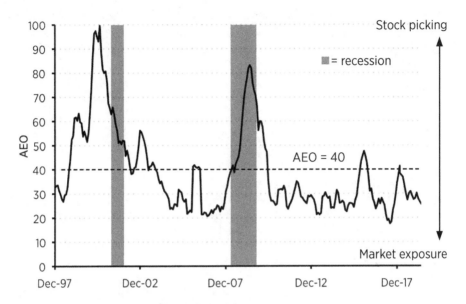

Sources: Morningstar and AthenaInvest.

Of interest is that since 2010, AEO has mostly been below average, declining to an all-time low of 18 in mid-2017. It since rebounded to 41 in February 2018, falling to 28 in January 2019.

The grey shaded areas represent NBER (National Bureau of Economic Research, the official arbitrator of business-cycle turning points) recessions. While there seems to be a relationship between recessions and higher levels of AEO, von Reibnitz, based on a longer 1972 through 2013 fund sample, concludes that, "… the positive relation between fund activeness and performance is driven by return dispersion, as opposed to business cycle fluctuations." That is, the impact of AEO on stock picking is largely independent of where we are in the business cycle.

Figure 5.5: Stock picking benefits vs AEO

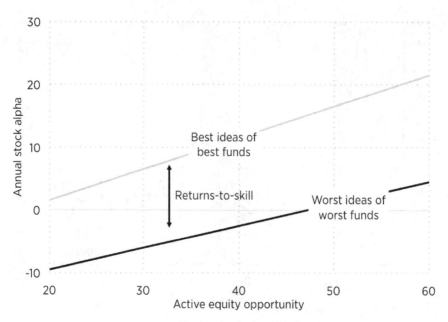

Alpha is stock return net of the Fama & French monthly market returns available on Ken French's website. Includes all stocks held by at least five active equity mutual funds in each month from January 1998 through May 2017. Sample comprises about half of the stocks traded on US exchanges each month and tens of millions of stock-fund-month observations. The reported results are the two regression lines when a month's best stocks' (and, separately, worst stocks) average alphas are regressed on month-beginning AEOs. The 20 to 60 range captures 85% of the observed AEO monthly values during this time period. Data sources: Morningstar and AthenaInvest.

Stock-picking skill is robust, but returns are not

Figure 5.5 presents the impact of AEO on stock alpha of the best idea stocks of the best funds (i.e., truly active as described previously) versus the worst ideas of the worst funds (i.e., closet indexers). The best (about 10% of all stocks held by active equity funds) are those most held by strategy-consistent, high-conviction funds, while the worst are those most held by strategy-inconsistent, low-conviction funds. Best and worst idea stocks are identified by aggregating fund relative holdings.

Skill benefits remain strong even at low levels of AEO, with differences averaging over 10%, confirming that funds can distinguish good from bad investment ideas. Skill benefits increase as AEO increases, reaching 15% at AEO of 60. So, stock-picking skill exists no matter the current state of the economy and the market.

However, as AEO drops, more and more stocks held by funds generate negative alpha. At AEO of 20, only the best ideas (top 10%) generate positive alpha while the other 90% sport a negative alpha. Thus, even best funds, those that focus most on high conviction stocks, can underperform when AEO is low, despite their investment team's stock picking prowess. This comports with the anecdotal evidence that stock picking is effective in certain markets while not in others.

Those searching for the best investment managers, including those hiring asset manager teams, should keep in mind that a low AEO environment reduces returns to stock picking skill. In this situation, even skilled managers my not be able to outperform.

Chapter review and what is to come

The evidence is overwhelming that past performance is not predictive of future fund performance. However, virtually everyone, including professionals and individuals alike, rely primarily on past performance when choosing funds in which to invest.

If instead you want to have the best chance of selecting a fund that will outperform, your focus should be on the fund manager's behavior. Invest in those funds that consistently pursue a narrowly-defined strategy while taking high-conviction positions.

Active equity funds can identify their best-idea stocks, to ex-ante rank by future performance, and to weight them accordingly in the portfolio. Therefore, care should be taken to avoid restricting a manager's ability to invest in their best ideas. This means abandoning the idea of minimizing style drift, tracking error, and volatility, as well as not growing the fund too large. Each of these represent impediments to focusing on best ideas. Let them be free to *roam* about the equity universe in the consistent of their narrowly-defined strategy.

Returns to stock picking skill vary based on market conditions, with the cross-sectional volatility of individual stock returns being the best predictor.

We now turn to the harnessing of big data for building and managing portfolios.

Chapter 6.
Prescriptions for Quantitative Analysis

Unearthing profitable strategies

AFTER A LONG struggle, Bruce Bennett decided to leave his position as an analyst for a large investment platform and turn his attention to building strategies that can generate superior returns for end clients.

Having interviewed many mutual and hedge fund investment teams in his former job, he was aware of the skill and resources needed to evaluate and select individual securities. He felt it was likely difficult to gather the primary information upon which many of these teams base their analyses. Instead he decided to focus on the large secondary data sets available within the investment industry. Being a quantitative person at heart, this approach appealed to him.

While huge amounts of market and individual data were available, he was aware that big data alone does not a successful strategy make. There are hundreds of documented anomalies upon which to build a strategy. This very fact was why he recently rejected the EMH. But there was a widespread belief that many anomalies were the consequence of data mining by using powerful statistical packages to snoop around giant data sets. This was thought to yield questionable, non-replicable results.

And even if the measured returns were true, the strategies delivering them were sure to be arbitraged away once they became widely known.

Behavioral price distortions

Bruce ventured further into the unknown and focused on the pricing errors driven by the collective behavioral mistakes of investors. He planned to employ large data sets to unearth measurable and persistent mistakes upon which to build a strategy. Bruce wanted to identify the specific behavior behind the distortions he was trying to harness. He also had to consider how likely the behavior was to change, as well as how easily the opportunity could be arbitraged away by funds and investors specializing in exploiting the distortion.

Philosophically, this meant Bruce had to move away from the more traditional MPT-based assumption of ascribing price movements to changes in underlying fundamentals. Instead, in his new approach, fundamentals and other objective information played a behind-the-scenes role as proxies for collective investor behavior.

With these thoughts in mind, Bruce set about building his behavioral investment strategies.

* * *

The world is awash in big data and managers are using it evermore in their investment activities. Many investment teams use secondary big data to augment their efforts at gathering primary data. Academics use broad, long-time-period data sets for testing models based on economic first principles, such as profit and expected utility maximization, as well as for testing reported pricing anomalies. Others use powerful computer programs to search for patterns that can be used to earn superior returns. In this chapter we will discuss how to harness big data for building successful investment strategies.

Building an investment strategy

A fundamental analyst is often assigned a specific sector or industry, so the possible investment ideas are limited to those assigned. In the case of big data/behavioral investing, the possible ideas are wide open. They can emerge from news reports, academic and practitioner articles, discussions with other professionals, webinars, conference presentations, and from many other sources. An open mind is important since the next best idea may be something that had not crossed your mind before.

The resulting ideas are those driven by an identifiable behavioral factor and thus can lead you in a wide variety of directions. Typically, there is a pipeline of such ideas in different stages of development and implementation. This will produce a range of portfolio offerings whose only common feature is that they are behaviorally driven.

Idea testing

Testing these ideas may require gathering primary data that is available publicly, but not yet aggregated into a commercial database. Once aggregated it is referred to as secondary data. The advantage of secondary data is that it is often possible to create large cross-sectional, long-period longitudinal data sets. For example, it is possible to create a data set involving multiple data points for thousands of individual stocks over hundreds of months. This can result in hundreds of thousands, if not millions, of observations.

Once the database is assembled, statistical testing can begin. The goal is to confirm the investment idea works over a diverse set of situations and over as long a period as possible. It often makes sense to confirm your findings by consulting academic papers that have tested similar ideas.[68] Frequently you will be able to find several papers that have explored the idea you are testing. An important advantage of this approach is that academic studies are required to conduct numerous robustness tests to determine if the results hold up in a variety of circumstances. This means that you do not have to conduct such extensive testing.

Different aspects of the planned investment strategy should be tested as investors, consultants and analysts will ask if you have considered alternative approaches. For example, it is not uncommon to use moving averages for implementing an investment strategy and the period for calculating the average will be questioned. It is good practice to test different period lengths so that this question can be addressed when it arises.

Statistical versus economic significance

Of course, there is no guarantee that the initial investment idea works. The ideal result is to find one that is both statistically and economically significant. If the idea turns out to be economically insignificant, it should be rejected even if it is statistically significant. The situation in which the idea is economically significant but statistically insignificant is not as straightforward.

---

[68] Academic working papers, as well as published articles, can be obtained at Social Sciences Research Network (www.ssrn.com).

When big data is combined with a powerful statistical package the problem of data mining and snooping can arise. As is jokingly pointed out, the US stock market is correlated with the number of camels in Afghanistan. Correlation does not necessarily imply usefulness or causality. Unfortunately, one can generate many high correlations with a lot of data. Deciding which of these are useable is the challenge.

The typical solution is to specify a value an estimate must exceed to be declared statistically significant. We prefer using the t-value statistic, which is the ratio of the estimate to its standard error.[69] If the t-value is large enough, then with some level of confidence we can say that our result is not due to chance. That is, the estimate rises above the considerable randomness that is inherent in financial markets. This randomness often makes possible the opportunities we are seeking but, on the other hand, it is the statistical bane in our efforts to uncover them.

To come up with a t-value it is necessary to calculate an estimate along with its corresponding standard error, based on sample observations. The standard error represents the range of estimates we can expect due to underlying randomness. For example, if we estimate a strategy can outperform the market by 5% annually (the estimate) with a standard error of 3.5%, then we are 95% confident that the true value lies between –1% and 11%, which is plus and minus two standard errors around the estimate, assuming a normal distribution for the estimate. Its t-value is calculated as 1.43 (= 5 / 3.5).

---

[69] There are other statistics used to gauge significance, including p-value (the probability that the t-value exceeds a specified value), F-square (multiple variable t-value test), and others. In each case, the goal is to determine if the estimate is large enough to not be the result of random chance.

Separating the signal from the noise

An important consideration is determining the amount by which the estimate must differ from zero, relative to its standard error, to be statistically significant. In other words, how far away from the mean, as measured by the number of standard errors, is the estimate. Simply stated, how strong is this signal amongst the random noise?

A widely accepted threshold is the t-value must be greater than 2.0 (or less than -2.0 if the estimate is negative). So, the 5% excess return above would not be considered statistically significant, since its t-value is only 1.43.

The t-value threshold is not as objective as it first appears. Because of randomness, it is impossible to say with certainty that an estimate is different from zero. For each estimate, it is always possible that the true value is zero even though the t-value exceeds the threshold (referred to as a false positive), or the true value is positive when the t-value is insignificant (referred to as a false negative). Traditional statistical analysis sets the threshold at 2.0 in order to reduce false positives at the expense of false negatives. In other words, we prefer to reject a strategy that works rather than accept one that doesn't.

When the t-value threshold is set at 2.0, we are taking a 5% chance of accepting a strategy that in fact does not work, since 5% of possible values are greater than 2 standard errors from the estimate, based on the typical assumption of a normal distribution of estimates. But on the other hand, we are rejecting many strategies that work but have insignificant t-values based on the threshold of 2.0. The only way to reduce the rejection of profitable strategies is to increase the acceptance of those that don't work. You can think of this as a sliding scale. As the threshold is increased further above 0, more profitable strategies are rejected while fewer unprofitable strategies are accepted. At the extreme threshold, all strategies, whether profitable or not, are rejected.

Determining economic significance

Of critical importance is the economic significance of the estimate. Is the estimated return large enough to cover portfolio management costs and thus generate superior returns? A relationship that promises to beat a benchmark by 10 bp annually may be statistically significant but not worth the effort of building an investment methodology. Each investment team must determine the performance improvement needed to justify further development, or, in other words, the level of economic significance required.

Consider the example above. The 5% excess return is clearly economically significant, but it is not statistically significant. In an academic research setting, the result would be declared statistically insignificant and rejected. But in a strategy development setting the answer is not so clear cut. Could this be a false negative? If so, an opportunity that might beat the market by 5% should not be abandoned.

Strong economic significance may justify lowering the traditional t-value threshold. There are no specific criteria for deciding when economic significance trumps statistical insignificance – rather the trade-off will be up to each investment team. Thus, it may make sense to move forward with an idea that is economically significant even though, by traditional standards, it is judged to be statistically insignificant.

Other statistical matters

Recently, Campbell Harvey, Yan Liu, and Heqing Zhu argued that many of the over 300 anomalies identified in the academic literature are interrelated and therefore the t-value statistical significance threshold should be raised from the typical 2 to 3 or even higher.[70] While they provide statistical arguments for such a change, the downside is that an increasing number of profitable strategies will be rejected as a result. Their suggestion is more relevant for the academic community. The economic significance versus statistical insignificance trade-off facing those building investment strategies remains, albeit maybe with a modified t-value acceptance value. By the way, Harvey, Liu, and Zhu find that half of the 300 anomalies remain statistically significant even if the higher threshold of 3 is applied.

A final thing to keep in mind with big data is that even the weakest of relationships can turn out to be statistically significant, since standard errors are inversely related to the square root of the number of sample observations. As standard error declines, statistical significance increases. Tests based on large samples of monthly, daily and tick-by-tick data can lead to highly statistically significant results, with small coefficients looming large relative to much smaller standard errors. In this situation, statistical significance is meaningless and only economic significance matters.

Building an investment methodology

Once the idea is validated, the process of building an investment methodology around this idea can begin. This includes deciding on the

---

[70]   Campbell R. Harvey, Yan Liu and Heqing Zhu, '... and the Cross-Section of Expected Returns', *The Review of Financial Studies* 29:1 (2016), pp. 5–68.

specific buy and sell signals, the securities to be used, and the trading protocol. One of the more important things that can be developed is an objective selling rule. The most common mistake made by professional investors is selling based on emotional attachment. This error can be reduced or eliminated entirely by creating carefully researched objective selling rules.

The arbitrage challenge

Once an idea has been accepted and a strategy built, the problem going forward is performance erosion due to arbitrage. Once implemented, it is possible that others will begin pursuing the same strategy and by trading alongside you it can reduce or even eliminate the opportunity uncovered in earlier research.

Proponents of the efficient market hypothesis contend that such arbitrage-motivated trading means all superior return opportunities are eventually eliminated. Actual evidence paints a much more nuanced picture.

Pure arbitrage occurs when a synthetic T-Bill can be created using various investment instruments and then combined with a long (or short) actual T-Bill. If prices of the actual and synthetic T-Bills are not equal, a risk-free, guaranteed profit is possible. Arbitrageurs respond quickly. Thus, pure arbitrage opportunities are only available to the largest and fastest participants, so most investors cannot profit from these price distortions.

An example is the pure arbitrage opportunity underlying the well-known Black-Scholes option pricing model. When continuously writing the correct number of calls and at the same time holding the underlying security, a synthetic T-Bill emerges. Financing this position with a short T-Bill creates a guaranteed profit if the security, option, and T-Bill prices are not correctly priced. Since all three instruments are highly liquid, this opportunity is quickly arbitraged away.[71]

Risky arbitrage

But this powerful model has its limitations. While at-the-money (i.e., current security price is close to the option exercise price) option premiums conform to Black-Scholes predictions, deep out-of-the-money options do not, referred to as the option smile. The Black-Scholes model significantly underestimates these premiums due to the possibility of large price jump events that cannot be easily modelled. So deep out-of-the-money options cannot be used to create a synthetic T-Bill and so there is no longer a pure arbitrage available – rather, it becomes a risky one.

As the name implies, risky arbitrage involves taking on short-term investment risk, thus is less effective in eliminating price distortions. Almost all so-called arbitrage in the financial markets is risky, save for a few situations in the options, currency, and other markets. While it is possible investor arbitrage activity will eliminate price distortions, it is not very likely. Arbitrageurs as a group are looking for close to pure opportunities, so when these opportunities turn risky, investor interest wanes. For most potential arbitrageurs, if it takes days, weeks, or months to reap the gain, they become increasingly uninterested in pursuing the opportunity.

---

[71] Legend has it that prior to being published in 1973, Black and Scholes traded mispriced options based on their model. The model was quickly adopted by market participants and so the easy pickings disappeared shortly after publication.

David McLean and Jeffrey Pontiff examined the market's ability to eliminate return anomalies. If arbitrage is effective, then when anomalies are made public via academic publication, the superior returns should disappear. But they found that of the 82 anomalies they studied, the average post-publication excess return decay was 35%, meaning investor pressure eliminated only a third of these returns.[72]

Why were these attractive returns not fully eliminated?

A large body of academic research has explored this question and identified the state of the market along with security characteristics that make arbitrage difficult and expensive to pursue. These are referred to as limits to arbitrage (LTA). To date, the LTAs that have been uncovered include higher market sentiment,[73] lower institutional stock ownership, greater idiosyncratic risk, small number of stocks available for short sale, low trading liquidity, high transactions costs, smaller stocks, low profitability, non-dividend paying, and greater financial distress.

As can be seen, there are numerous LTAs standing in the way of fully eliminating price anomalies, or what we refer to as behavioral price distortions. There is every reason to believe that LTAs will continue to exist into the foreseeable future.

---

[72]   David R. McLean and Jeffrey Pontiff, 'Does Academic Research Destroy Stock Return Predictability?', *Journal of Finance* 71:1 (2015), pp. 3–32.

[73]   The most useful sentiment index is one created by Malcolm Baker and Jeffrey Wurgler, 'Investor Sentiment in the Stock Market', *Journal of Economic Perspectives* (2007), pp. 129–151. Rather than relying on typical sentiment surveys, their index is based on six measures capturing actual investor decisions. That is, *put your money where your mouth is* measures rather than *what investors say* measures.

Here's why

After being statistically and economically verified, an investment idea has a good chance of continuing to work once implemented. The wider the LTA moat surrounding the opportunity, the more likely it is to survive. There is a rationale for why each LTA exists. For several, investor emotions are the primary reason. To be successful as an investment manager you must not view the LTAs defending your portfolio in the same way as do arbitrageurs. That is, where they are unwilling to tread, you rush in to reap returns. In the broadest sense, you continuously hold a contrary view of markets and securities and take opposite positions from those who shy away from emotional triggers.

Another important LTA is driven by trading frequency. Many investors prefer a manager (which could be themselves) who closely follows market and individual security events and makes decisions quickly. This appeals to our brain's inherent impatience, the source of the cognitive errors known as the fallacy of information and fallacy of control.[74]

For this reason, short time period trading (hours, days, weeks) is unlikely to generate superior returns, since they are often crowded trades. Like the approach with other LTAs, it is good to avoid the trading frequency most inhabited by others. While it is hard to generalize, when building our strategies, we often find that trading every six months to a year works best. This is long enough to avoid the crowded short-term trades but frequent enough to take advantage of changing economic and market conditions.

---

[74] The many DIY investing ads that populate all forms of media provide evidence of the pervasiveness of these emotional drivers. Our favorite one has a baby making investment decisions in his crib using the advertiser's online information and trading software!

Building an investment strategy: constant volatility

Constant volatility (CV) is an investment strategy in which portfolio trades are driven by current volatility measures. CV is based on varying exposure inversely to current volatility. For example, if volatility is half its historical average, the portfolio is levered 2×, while if it is twice its average, the portfolio is invested half in cash. Since this approach relies only on publicly available information and can be easily implemented, there should be no benefit for such a simple approach, as the excess returns should be arbitraged away.

However, Alan Moreira and Tyler Muir find that pursuing this strategy generates a 5% alpha for the US stock market portfolio. They also find superior returns can be earned on factor, bond, futures, and international portfolios as well.[75] It appears the usefulness of CV is widespread. Why does CV work so well in such a wide range of markets? Moreira and Muir note that investors are slow to adjust expected returns as volatility changes. Therefore, the inverse volatility strategy generates superior returns.[76]

But what LTA is preserving this opportunity? The use of leverage may be the key. There is a widespread behavioral aversion to the use of leverage in financial markets, both by institutional and individual investors. This is mostly for emotional reasons, but in many situations regulators and institutions ban the use of leverage in portfolios (regulations can create powerful LTAs!). This is the case for the large broker–dealer segment of the industry and as well as for many retirement and trust accounts. The

---

[75]   Alan Moreira and Tyler Muir, 'Volatility-Managed Portfolios', *The Journal of Finance* LXXII:4 (2017), pp. 1611–1644.
[76]   Pedro Barroso and Andrew Detzel show the leverage LTA is not explained by the institutional ownership and idiosyncratic volatility LTAs, 'Do Limits to Arbitrage Explain the Benefits of Volatility-Managed Portfolios', University of Denver Working Paper (2018).

leverage LTA is driven by the legal framework underlying the investment management industry and so is not likely to change any time soon.

The CV strategy is an idea that is both statistically and economically significant, so it is worth building an investment strategy around it. Furthermore, a strong LTA protecting this opportunity has been identified. The next step is to build a specific investment methodology.

A variation on constant volatility

It is not necessary to vary portfolio leverage based on volatility to take advantage of this opportunity for building long-horizon wealth. Buying and holding a 2× US stock market portfolio from January 1980 through December 2017 generated a 21.3% compound return, a return that is 9.5% greater than the unlevered version. A $10,000 initial investment in 1980 results in a final 2017 value of over $15m, compared to $680,000 for the unlevered portfolio![77]

Why don't investors pursue this highly profitable yet simple to implement strategy? One reason is the prohibition by many in the industry against using leverage, as mentioned above. Another is that the volatility of the 2× portfolio is much higher and investors respond emotionally to increased volatility.[78]

---

[77] Based on daily market returns available from Ken French's data library (mba.tuck.dartmouth.edu/pages/faculty/ken.french/data_library.html). The daily market return is calculated as the capitalization-weighted return for all stocks listed on the NYSE, AMEX, and NASDAQ. The 2× return is twice the daily return.

[78] The largest one-day 2× drop from 1980 through 2017 was 35% on Black Monday, October 19, 1987, while the largest 2× drawdown was 83% (versus 54% for the unlevered portfolio) from July 19, 2007 to March 9, 2009, during the Great Recession. Both events triggered strong emotions in investors and challenged

Not helping is the widespread use of performance metrics based on short-term volatility, such as the Sharpe ratio. The 2× Sharpe ratio does not show outperformance even though it outperforms the unlevered portfolio by 9.5%. Keep in mind that compound returns already account for the increased 2× volatility. The small compound return reduction due to increased 2× volatility drag is dwarfed by the large return contribution of using leverage.[79]

Relying on the Sharpe ratio, which is a ratio of compound return to short-term standard deviation, double counts the downside of increased volatility, emphasizing it well beyond its impact on the compound return. Because volatility triggers emotions and since this ratio encourages a focus on long-term return versus short-term volatility, investors shy away from the highly profitable use of leverage in investment portfolios.

Straightforward but emotionally difficult

The collective interplay among leverage, volatility, regulation, industry practices, and strong emotions produces a powerful leverage–volatility LTA. Strategies built around leverage and volatility price distortions have an excellent chance of working for a long time.

---

them to stay in their seats. Note that due to daily compounding, the portfolio's value will not drop to zero unless the one-day market loss exceeds 50%, something that has not come close to happening since 1926.

[79] As a rough guide, if the expected annual return is less than 3%, the 2× compound return can end up being less than the unlevered compound return. For a comprehensive analysis see Tony Cooper, 'Alpha Generation and Risk Smoothing using Managed Volatility', Working Paper (2010).

But many who look at this strategy will have numerous reasons, many emotional, why this strategy should not be pursued. As a manager implementing this strategy, you must not respond to the emotional triggers that pervade this portfolio. If you can do as such, you will be a member of a small group within the industry. But over 40 years, you will enjoy earning 20 times more than what those who invest the same amount in a buy-and-hold strategy.[80] And the strategy is simple to implement: buy-and-hold 2× the stock market![81]

Creating and managing this type of portfolio confirms the general observation that building superior portfolios is straightforward, but emotionally difficult.

Those searching for quantitative investment methods that are rooted in behavior and likely to persist successfully for a period of time, should understand the characteristics of the CV strategy – as defined above – and seek out other strategies that share these characteristics.

---

[80] We know even this is difficult to achieve as many investors bolt the stock market in the face of frequent drawdowns.

[81] It is even easier now to implement, as numerous 2× broad market ETFs exist, such as the 2× S&P 500 ETF with ticker SSO. Interestingly, broker dealers discourage and even ban the long-term holding of leveraged ETFs because they do not exactly track the underlying index on a daily basis. This is like taking a sledgehammer to a trivial problem, further reinforcing the already powerful leverage-volatility LTA. For evidence supporting the long-term holding of leveraged ETFs, see Anthony Loviscek, Hongfei Tang, Xiaoqing Eleanor Xu, 'Do leveraged exchange-traded products deliver their stated multiples?', *Journal of Banking and Finance* 43 (2014), pp. 29–47.

Using big data to build successful investment strategies

Are there successful applications of big data behavioral research? Indeed, there are. The funds we discuss below conduct big data research, with behavioral factors as their primary focus, relegating fundamental and technical factors to a secondary role, if considered at all.

Fuller & Thaler Asset Management

Founded in 1993, Fuller & Thaler Asset Management (FTAM) has pioneered the application of behavioral finance in investment management. Primarily focused on US small-cap equities, FTAM strategies have historically delivered exceptional results. More importantly, FTAM's process differs significantly from traditional equity managers.

At the individual stock level, FTAM searches for events that suggest investor misbehavior. Investors make mistakes. FTAM looks for them. There are two kinds of mistakes that produce buying opportunities: overreaction and underreaction. Other investors may overreact to bad news and losses (e.g., panic), or they may underreact to good news (e.g., not pay attention).

FTAM believes their unique perspective and unconventional approach can provide meaningful diversification to mutual fund and separate account clients. Today, the firm manages and advises on assets in excess of $9bn (as of March 2019) utilizing expertise in behavioral finance.

Werner De Bondt and Richard Thaler first reported on stock market overactions 35 years ago in *The Journal of Finance*.[82] FTAM's strategies are built on this carefully researched and persistent behavioral price distortion. Since FTAM has successfully managed their portfolios for 25 years, there must be a wide LTA moat surrounding the overreaction/underreaction behavioral distortion.[83]

AthenaInvest Behavioral Funds

The research effort upon which behavioral strategies are based began in 2005 by identifying the ten investment strategies, listed in the table below, being pursued by US and international active equity mutual funds in order to generate superior returns. Each strategy concentrates on a specific set of market factors.[84]

The resulting database is comprised of tens of millions of active equity mutual fund strategy returns, holdings and other data points, some going back as far as 40 years. This data captures the collective intelligence of 3000 active US and international fund managers. The challenge is to extract useful signals from this massive data set.[85]

---

[82] Werner F. M. De Bondt and Richard Thaler, 'Does the Stock Market Overreact?', *The Journal of Finance* 40:3 (1985), pp. 793–805.

[83] For more, visit: www.fullerthaler.com/funds

[84] See Tom's paper, 'The Importance of Investment Strategy' (2010), for details on how strategy information is used to form strategy peer groups.

[85] Several useful concepts have emerged from strategy database research. These include objective measures of desirable active equity fund behaviors (strategy consistency while taking large high conviction positions), strategy stock pools, best stock ideas of the best manager, and market barometers, discussed in the next section. Each of these have led to investment products that outperform.

Figure 6.1: Strategy peer groups

Competitive Position	Business principles, including quality of management, market power, product reputation, and competitive advantage. Considers the sustainability of the business model and history of adapting to market changes.
Economic Conditions	Top down approach based on economic fundamentals: can include employment, productivity, inflation, and industrial output. Gauges where overall economy is in business cycle, the resulting supply and demand situations in various industries, and the best stocks to purchase as a result.
Future Growth	Companies poised to grow rapidly relative to others. The Future Growth and Valuation strategies are not mutually exclusive and can both be deemed important in the investment process.
Market Conditions	Consideration of stock's recent price and volume history relative to the market and similar stocks as well as the overall stock market conditions.
Opportunity	Unique opportunities that may exist for a small number of stocks or at different points in time. May involve combining stocks and derivatives and may involve use of considerable leverage. Many hedge fund managers follow this strategy, but a mutual fund manager may also be so classified.
Profitability	Company profitability, such as gross margin, operating margin, net margin and return on equity.
Quantitative	Mathematical and statistical inefficiencies in market and individual stock pricing. Involves mathematical and statistical modeling with little or no regard to company and market fundamentals.
Risk	Control overall risk, with increasing returns a secondary consideration. Risk measures considered may include beta, volatility, company financials, industry and sector exposures, country exposures, and economic and market risk factors.

Social Considerations	Company's ethical, environmental, and business practices as well as an evaluation of the company's business lines in light of the current social and political climate. A manager can look for these criteria or the lack of in selecting an stock.
Valuation	Stocks selling cheaply compared to peer stocks based on accounting ratios and valuation techniques. The Valuation and Future Growth strategies are not mutually exclusive and can both be deemed important in the investment process.

Figure 6.2: Strategy ranks and expected market returns

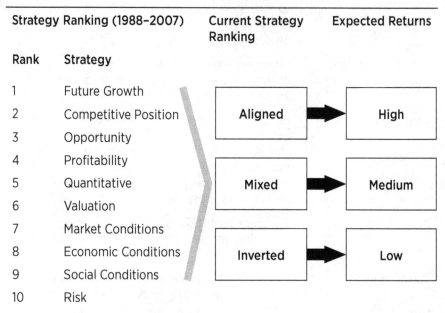

Strategy Ranking (1988–2007)		Current Strategy Ranking	Expected Returns
Rank	Strategy		
1	Future Growth		
2	Competitive Position	Aligned	High
3	Opportunity		
4	Profitability		
5	Quantitative	Mixed	Medium
6	Valuation		
7	Market Conditions		
8	Economic Conditions	Inverted	Low
9	Social Conditions		
10	Risk		

Measuring deep behavioral currents

Athena's very successful Global Tactical SMA is based on the monthly ranking of strategy index returns. It turns out these recent ranks, relative to long-term ranks, is predictive of future overall market returns.

Extensive statistical analysis over the period 1980–2010 revealed that this predictability was both economically and statistically significant.[86]

Figure 6.2 provides a graphical representation of the relationship between strategy ranks and expected market returns. If current strategy ranks align with long-term ranks, then expected returns are high. This means investors are currently favoring strategies in the same order they have performed over the long run. More specifically, investors are favoring Future Growth stocks and Competitive Position stocks. This is a positive sign for the market and leads to expected returns well above the 10% long-term average.

Conversely, if ranks are inverted in relationship to long-term ranks, investors instead are rewarding Risk, Social Considerations, Economic Conditions and Market Conditions stocks, which are historically weaker strategies. This is a bad sign for the market because it indicates investors are taking a defensive posture rather than focusing on long-term stock market drivers. As a result, the expected market return is weak or even negative. For example, Social Considerations, Risk, and Market Conditions were top relative strategies in 2008, a bad sign for the market. And we know what happened in 2008.

Strategy ranks most often fall in between aligned and inverted and, as a result, the expected market return of the US stock market is somewhere around the long-term average of 10%. Strategy ranks are calculated separately for developed global markets and US markets and each has proven effective in capturing macro-level crowd behavior.[87]

---

[86]   These tests are reported in Tom's paper, 'Behavioral Estimates of Expected Market Return' (2010).

[87]   For more, visit: www.athenainvest.com

Which firms are doing this?

Fuller & Thaler and AthenaInvest are just two firms that have successfully implemented big data behavioral investment strategies in each of their portfolio offerings. There are other fund families that have one or more behaviorally-focused funds.

One of the more successful is the 361 US Small Cap Equity Fund managed by John Riddle. Based on 30 years of research, the Fund's quantitative process taps into behavioral biases to identify stocks poised for appreciation. Believing security prices are influenced by the opinion of perceived experts and that the behavior of these experts follows a predictable pattern, this fund invests in companies that are likely to be the beneficiaries of future favorable earnings announcements and earnings estimate revisions.[88]

Chapter review and what is to come

Big data provides opportunities to build superior strategies based on investor behavior, but the effort is bedevilled by the considerable randomness pervading financial markets. An investment idea must be carefully researched before a decision is made to move on to methodology construction. Necessary research includes tests using the largest cross-sectional, longest-period sample possible. The sample may include both primary and secondary data, with the latter more easily producing a large diverse sample.

---

[88] John Riddle, 'Bounded Rationality: Tapping Investor Behavior to Source Alpha', 361 Capital White Paper (2017). For more, visit: www.361capital.com/all-products/361-u-s-small-cap-equity-fund

Initial tests focus on the economic and statistical significance of the returns, relative to a benchmark, generated by implementing the idea. Economic significance, that is a return sufficiently higher than the benchmark, is required in order to build a strategy around it. The best is if statistical significance is also high, but there may be good reasons to move forward with an idea that is economically significant, but not so statistically. Another issue is that with huge databases, even the smallest advantage becomes statistically significant. In this case, only economic significance matters.

Once the strategy is built, attention turns to performance degradation due to arbitrage. Most desirable is a strategy protected by a wide LTA (limits to arbitrage) moat. There are market conditions, security characteristic, and trading frequency LTAs that allow a strategy to continue working into the foreseeable future. Some are driven by fundamentals and others by regulators, but most are the result of collective emotional decisions made by investors. To be a successful manager, it is necessary to not respond to these LTAs in the same way as do most investors and consistently pursue the strategy considering the inevitable criticism from clients and others.

Beyond creating a wide LTA moat, a strategy can only continue to work if it is offered by a firm committed to making it work. In the next chapter we focus on the behavioral investment firm that can make this a reality.

Chapter 7.
Prescriptions for Managing the Active Investment Management Firm

Importance of firm structure

WANTING YANG WAS attending a presentation by a fund manager who had just been anointed Fund Manager of the Decade by Morningstar. She was all ears listening to him describe his way of delivering outsized results.

The manager said, "I wake up very early and digest the news from many different news sites. I check my email for news alerts about the companies we own in the portfolio. I read the regulatory releases of each firm front cover to back cover. I conduct financial statement analysis and build discounted cash flow valuation models. I interview management and conduct on-site research as well as my own independent research." And so on.

Wanting had accomplished her long-held goal of becoming a portfolio manager, garnering superior returns in recent years. She had recently become interested in what kind of fund structure leads to managers producing their best investment performance. The Manager of the Decade presentation further piqued her interest.

The investment firm difference

Wanting knew from her own anecdotal investigations that many investment managers did not do all of the above that the ace manager described. However, she also recognized that there was nothing secret about the manager's process. Based on her experience as a high-performing investment manager, she knew that an important difference was having a firm culture that supported the execution of the fund's investment strategy without obstacles put in place by the firm.

From talking to fellow research analysts and fund managers over the years, Wanting knew just how difficult it could be to implement and execute a strategy that is at odds with the firm's values and structure. Said another way, investment firms often get in the way of their funds.

When Wanting asked the Fund Manager of the Decade how important a supportive firm level culture and structure was to his success, the manager replied, "Oh my gosh, that's everything."

Firm structure matters

Thus far we have discussed in *ROAM* the overall strategy of investment management (MPT vs behavioral finance) and the new tools available when moving to a behavioral focus. However, both of us believe that the structure of investment management firms, as well as firm-level decisions, also play a large role in the success of investment analysts.

Yet, only infrequently is this ever discussed by academic researchers or practitioners. Simply stated, firms must support funds and their research staff in order to maximize their ability to earn excess returns for end clients.

Most investment management firms have many different departments executing many different functions. All too often these different departments operate in isolation from one another, with intra-firm rivalries, recriminations, and resentments. Or firms see the non-portfolio management aspects as business expenses rather than as revenue generators. Or firms have never taken the time to get these other departments right. These unnecessary frictions typically have a fund-level manifestation that hurts investment performance, and consequently firm performance, too.

Aligning key interests

To unleash the power of research analysts and portfolio managers, firms need to carefully align themselves internally with the board of directors, marketing, information technology, and performance reporting.

Board of directors

At most firms, the board of directors is not supportive of periods of underperformance from investment managers. Boards can be just as impatient as investors with poor performance – after all, the board works for the shareholders. Consequently, firms need to spend time educating their boards about the underlying investment philosophies of their products and the time it takes to realize the fruits of them. Additionally, when recruiting new board members, assuming investment decision-makers have a say in such matters, it makes sense to find those who are committed to serving the best execution of the underlying investment strategy. This attitude puts shareholders of the individual funds first and considerations at the investment firm level second.

It may sound as if we are advocating boards of directors stacked with sympathetic insiders, but we are not. We believe even independent boards would like to be liberated from conversations at quarterly board meetings that do not serve the end shareholder. Instead, if the investment strategy of individual funds is clearly stated, the expectations of board responsibilities are well established, and the board's culture is aligned with the investment strategy, then an independent board is freer to focus on what matters: execution of the strategy in service to shareholders.

Without this alignment of interests and understanding between asset managers and the board, these two critical forces can unnecessarily obstruct one another in the fulfillment of their duties. Unfortunately, it is the end investor that suffers the most in this environment.

We propose:

- Asking the board for time at a quarterly meeting to ensure that it understands the investment philosophy and strategy of individual funds.

- Sharing with the board the history of how returns are typically earned by quality investment managers; typically, it is over longer periods of time.

- Ensuring the board knows that all active investment managers underperform some of the time.

- Making board meetings not just about a review of buys and sells in the quarter, but about active investment manager feedback about the opportunity sets available to the research staff, and perceptions about how the fund should perform.

- Boards develop other ways of evaluating the success of managers that are not simply performance-driven, or the broken metrics of Sharpe ratios, tracking error, and style drift.

- Boards ask active investment managers pointed questions about how they continually adapt to the ever-changing global economy and market conditions.

Sales and marketing

Our experience is that the members of investment management firms' sales departments are typically compensated by commissions or other sales-type incentives. Unwittingly, they are also incentivized to earn the next dollar of assets under management (AUM) without respect to whether that new client fully understands or supports the underlying investment strategy. This can only end badly for all parties.

If the sales department is working with wire houses primarily then, yes, you get scale in your AUM growth quickly, but you get very little chance of ensuring the end investor trusts the managers to execute the investment strategy over time. Wire houses have their own messages, and they typically are highly simplistic and of the form of 'this manager fits this style' or 'this manager has performed at the top,' whither the actual strategy of the research analysts and portfolio managers.

In the long run, this means that if the investment environment cuts against the grain of the strategy, assets under management can leave just as quickly as they came in. This is because the monies never came to the firm because of a strategy diligently executed, but for returns. In many cases, the aggrieved and ignorant clients never come back, or it is many years until they are open to investing with the fund manager again.

While wholesalers engage in direct sales prospects, many firms also have indirect marketing efforts. But most firms' advertising is identical in tone and type to that of the wire house where style and returns are advertised. Another popular choice, more recently in vogue circa 2018, is the advertising that is future oriented. Here the advertising shows clients' fulfilling their dreams – a retirement home, a sail boat, or exotic travel – by presumably having invested with the firm in question. This is better advertising in some ways, but more important for the research analysts and portfolio managers is not another dollar of liquidity to try and invest courtesy of more AUM, but that the end client understands the strategy and has bought into it before buying into the fund.

What we propose is that investment firms' sales and marketing departments:

- Be extremely well educated about the underlying investment philosophies represented by the firm's products.

- Be compensated not just for securing new AUM, but for the longevity of those assets under management, both at the individual, as well as wire house level.

- Be supported by the management and board so that the fund is able to turn away assets under management that are not aligned with the investment strategy. Furthermore, many marketing teams are looked down upon by the research staff, with wholesalers, for example, having very little access to the analysts and portfolio managers. This condescension is counterproductive to long-term wealth creation for end clients.

Performance reporting

How can an investment firm's performance reporting help the research staff? We know this may seem strange at first, but we promise we have not lost our minds. To us it is a lost opportunity if a portion of the performance staff is not trained to be able to help the research staff ask, and have answered, their questions about process and performance. In other words, those logging performances should be able to provide critical insights about contributors to/subtractors from performance.

In Jason's investment management career, performance reporting provided an end-of-the-day snapshot about performance relative only to the fund's chosen benchmark. Other than logging and recording x basis points up, down, or unchanged relative to the benchmark, there was no content. Recognizing that the ability to understand strategy and performance was key to continual improvement, Jason requested individual asset-level details about performance. He then created a comprehensive spreadsheet that provided, yes, a daily record of performance, but also a multi-period performance analysis extending out to the life of the fund. These insights helped Jason to improve the fund's performance. He scoured these reports for evidence of his own behavioral biases, for new lessons and insights that could turn into better analytical tools going forward, for repeated mistakes, and so on.

It is our belief that most firms do not have dedicated professionals helping research analysts and portfolio managers get better on a daily basis. If there is a mechanism in place, it is usually just a thorough report and is not a person who understands investment performance and who can ad hoc answer sophisticated questions, such as: "Do we exit technology stocks too early?" Imagine how different active management could be with this additional perspective.

Some firms even employ coaches for their research staff, as well as continuing professional development activities to help these harried folks become better at what they do. All of this begins with better performance reporting.

What we propose:

- Have someone on staff earn the Certificate in Investment Performance Management (CIPM) and empower this person with time and resources to assess fund performance.

- Hire someone with the CIPM designation.

- Encourage research analysts and portfolio managers to construct their own assessment tools to provide insights about how value is added: security selection, portfolio construction, risk avoidance, low-cost trading, proper timing of buys and sells, evidence of behavioral bias, and repeated mistakes.

Important firm-level decisions

It isn't just the structure and aligning key interests of the firm that needs to change to unleash the full firepower of investment professionals. Investment companies have many other important levers that they may pull to improve results.

Elevate buy-side investment analysts

The path we advocate in this book needs torchbearers – those who are committed to helping end clients achieve their goals. What better group of people than buy-side research analysts and portfolio managers?

It is these individuals who filter the universe of possible securities, purchasing or shorting assets, and building portfolios through their execution of investment strategies. They are on the frontlines, earning for both end clients and for their firms, and they need elevation.

Going forward, their traditional preeminent role in security selection and portfolio management needs to be restored. For too long, their skills have been undermined by portfolio management guided not by an investment strategy, but by investment intermediaries – consultants, platform gatekeepers, and investment committees. These intermediaries want managers to complete niche style boxes to fulfill a certain asset allocation. In other words, portfolio management is too much a product and needs to return to being a profession.

Naysayers may contend that those whom we hope to elevate are the very people who should be demoted. But until someone proves that intermediaries actually help clients achieve their end goals, there is no reason to discount the expertise of fundamental analysts. Buy-side analysts are quite adept at security selection, according to research by Tom and others.[89]

Focus on high-conviction stocks

Studies show that buy-side analysts are quite good at security selection. Take, for example, the high levels of accretive alpha of buy-side analysts' largest positions, for which they presumably have the greatest conviction, and as measured by ex ante relative portfolio

---

[89] C. Thomas Howard, 'Collective Intelligence Market Model', SSRN Working Paper (2015).

weights.[90] It is not a leap of faith to conclude that this conviction is based on a thorough understanding of individual securities, and a thorough analytical process having been applied to the security, too. In fact, moving down the relative weights of securities in a portfolio, performance worsens, with holdings beyond the top 20 generating negative alpha. In other words, most portfolios are over-diversified and research shows that this hurts performance.

Yet, most investment management firms have bought into the distribution system's unjustified preference for a high number of securities in portfolios as a way of minimizing *risk*, despite its deleterious effects on alpha. Firms, therefore, must ensure that analysts' high conviction in individual securities is honoured and reflected in individual portfolios. There are any number of ways of ensuring this outcome.

One way is to adjust the firm's culture so that only high conviction positions compose portfolios. Another way is to teach the marketing department how to talk to an investment management firm's stakeholders about the importance of high conviction to earning better returns. It is also likely that boards of directors also need to be educated about the importance of high conviction position taking.

Having only high conviction positions creates a problem for the successful manager who receives large investment flows when performance is good. Due to legislative requirements like the US Investment Company Act of 1940, maximum position sizes, applied to a portfolio's largest holdings – as measured by cost basis – force

---

[90]   Randoph B. Cohen, Christopher Polk, and Bernhard Silli, 'Best Ideas', Harvard Working Paper (2010).

managers to invest in securities in which they have less conviction.[91] For more on this see below, 'Do not asset bloat'.

Tom's research demonstrates that most fund managers are poorly diversified – as in overly so.[92] His research estimates that every one-decile increase of over-diversification subtracts 13.5 basis points (bps) from performance. Also, the research finds that for every one-decile increase in closet-indexing, that performance is negatively affected by a whopping 31.6 bps. So, as a manager's r-squared relative to their benchmark increases, performance decreases.

Do not asset bloat

Investment management firms need to reconsider business plans that preserve assets under management, but that deliver negative value to their end clients. More specifically, asset bloat, benchmark tracking, and over-diversification need to be discouraged. Why? Because these are the precursors to closet indexing. This system is clearly broken from the perspective of the investing public.

Instead funds need to be rewarded for consistently pursuing a narrowly-defined strategy in service to a well-defined philosophy, and consequently taking high-conviction positions. This is not just the responsibility of the investment management firm, as it requires that participants in the distribution ecosystem need to avoid imposing restrictions that impede the successful pursuit of an equity strategy. We believe we have

---

[91] 'Investment Company Act of 1940', Securities and Exchange Commission (rev. 2018).
[92] C. Thomas Howard, 'Why Most Equity Mutual Funds Underperform and How to Identify Those that Outperform', Advisor Perspectives (26 January 2016).

demonstrated that it is time to move past modern portfolio theory as the theoretical justification for many of the value-destroying restrictions foisted upon funds.

Furthermore, managers who invest in securities they don't believe in to avoid cash positions – remember that style drift problem! – should consider converting to an index fund if AUM grows too large. How large is too large? Tom's research suggests that AUM close to $1bn is too large for active equity funds.[93] Capping new inflows is also an option. Some funds do this to ensure that their security selection is built around high-conviction positions.

Do not benchmark track

Benchmarks were originally constructed to measure performance after the fact. Sadly, they have become targets for buy-side research analysts and portfolio managers to manage to before the fact.

To enforce this, investment intermediaries have developed measures – style boxes, style drift, and tracking error – that are entirely arbitrary. Why? Because, again, they want managers to adhere to a niche style box as part of an overarching asset allocation plan that is not typically subject to the same level of scrutiny.

Yet, Russ Wermers's work shows that active managers who comply with such foolishness will be beaten by indexes.[94] After all, active management

---

[93] Ibid.
[94] Russ Wermers, 'Matter of Style: The Causes and Consequences of Style Drift in Institutional Portfolios', University of Maryland Working Paper (2012).

should be about unleashing the capabilities of the human mind. Why rein these in with unnecessary requirements that destroy client value?

One way of overcoming this problem is to create benchmarks based on the actual strategy employed by an investment manager, as advocated in Chapter 5 in discussing 'Strategy Consistency'. Again, firms must be willing to change their internal culture in adherence to this idea, as well as be willing to try and change the expectations and understanding of the firm held by shareholders, asset owners, consultants, regulators, and so on.

Manage funds first, firms second

Results that wow are hard, but perhaps even harder is to unwind the modern fund complex. These are the collection of gigantic and often publicly-traded investment firms, some of which have hundreds of individual mutual funds.

These firms are managed at the firm level, not the fund level, meaning that individual investment management portfolios are just small assets in a larger portfolio. From the perspective of the firm and its shareholders, this may make sense. After all, a firm with 50-plus portfolios can probably deliver more consistent earnings-per-share growth for the fund parent and its shareholders. But for an individual investor in an individual fund, this usually means that they receive vanilla products that frequently deliver sour performance.

Why? Implicit in the fund complex business model is the assumption that a proportion of a firm's actively managed funds will be outperformers at any given time. The marketing department hypes these products to spur incremental earnings growth by attracting new AUM. Other products are offered as means to an asset allocation end:

> You bought us for the Superstar Fund, but intelligent investors also allocate assets to fixed income and to some cash. To ease your record-keeping burden and to keep all of your funds with us, we will offer you incentives (breakpoints) to purchase our other (mediocre) products.

Simply put, investment funds should be managed as investments first, and the firm should be managed second. That means the attraction of assets under management should first be about earning the returns needed to organically grow, rather than primarily about sales and marketing to grow AUM through acquisitions. It also means that individual funds should not be seen as assets under management, but instead as a promise to deliver to end clients. Likely the firm's incentive programs need to be reengineered, too.

Hiring, promoting, and compensating right

Hiring right

Many factors lead to a quality candidate. However, based on our years of experience there are really three overarching capabilities that the successful investment management professional needs:

1. To see the world for what it is and not what they would prefer it to be.

2. To be decisive with their understanding.

3. To be interested in learning and improving based on a continuous

evaluation of the source of successes and failures.

Clearly, these three skills are very different from one another, and to a great degree they demark the divide between the jobs of the research analyst and the portfolio manager.

Research analysts need to see the world for what it is, and not what they would prefer it to be. This is the beginning of quality research, and it specifically points out the role of behavioral bias and its importance to the investment process. This is also why hiring qualifies as a topic of conversation in a book about behavioral finance.

Portfolio managers also need the same skills as research analysts. However, to a much greater degree they are relied upon for investment decision-making and therefore they need decisiveness. Finally, all active investment managers need the gumption to adapt themselves to a constantly changing world.

What we propose:

- Hire those that have a unique viewpoint by interviewing for the level of creativity of a candidate; not just their ability to execute a discounted cash flow analysis. Ask what they do that is creative.

- Hire those that display a powerful curiosity, as measured by the breadth of subjects they know and their unusual interests. Ask what fascinates them.

- Hire those that show signs of introspection and self-knowledge because it is more likely they possess the fortitude and confidence necessary for being decisive. Ask about their process of self-discovery.

- Hire those who are self-motivated to learn and improve as a point of pride, not just because it is a requirement. Ask what they are currently interested in learning more about, and what have been their past research obsessions.

Promoting right

Investment management firms need to promote people based on how well they execute the responsibility of their jobs and not based on some arbitrary hierarchy that incentivizes propelling them up to the next rung on the ladder. For example, if a research analyst is best suited to work as a research analyst delivering 92nd percentile quality, why promote them to portfolio manager just to move them up the org chart or to give them a raise?

Instead, just give them a raise. In fact, expanding a successful manager's scope of duties may actually hurt subsequent performance.[95] Ditto: promoting portfolio managers to investment committees or chief investment officer just to provide more headroom for compensation.

There are also many behaviors that we believe contribute to success in the long run. We believe firms should begin to have hard targets for investment returns, but also soft targets that reflect professional development and longevity. In our last section we discussed some of the skills we believe are important for the ultimate success of a research analyst. Ensure that the demonstration of these qualities is a factor in performance evaluation and promotion.

---

[95] Richard B. Evans, Javier Gil-Bazo and Marc L. Lipson, 'Diseconomies of Scope and Mutual Fund Performance', Darden Business School Working Paper, No. 2874975 (2017), pp. 1–55.

Compensating right

It should be obvious that compensation should be on a time horizon that is in alignment with the time horizon of an investment strategy. We believe the bulk of pay should be time-weighted to long-term compensation. Yes, an annual bonus is worth paying, but higher pay should be available for better long-term results.

Why not structure compensation and benefits to reward excellence? In our vision, an exceptional research analyst could make more than an almost exceptional portfolio manager. Indeed, the typical analyst provides greater returns to a fund through stock-picking than does the typical portfolio manager through portfolio construction.[96] Of course, if people are evaluated correctly, then only those qualified as portfolio managers would be portfolio managers. Aligning minds and quality with work-type is key, don't you think?

This is true of other employees critical to investment management performance, too. Salespeople and marketers of firm products need to be promoted and compensated for delivering the correct investors to the firm, rather than just a quantity of investors to the firm. Imagine marketer pay that is based on the longevity of a vintage of money. Say a marketer brings $50m to an investment manager with a value orientation. Then the marketer ought to receive more long-term compensation for bringing in investors who stick around for longer periods of time, or whose clients ultimately increase their flows to the investment manager in down market periods, or who do not sell in the face of an equity market decline. In other words, we urge investment firms to become more creative in how they promote within their firms.

---

[96] Stefan Frey and Patrick Herbst, 'The Influence of Buy-Side Analysts on Mutual Fund Trading', SSRN (2014), pp. 1–40.

Also, marketers are frequently shut out of the C-suite, but if they deliver tremendous value to the firm then they should be eligible for such positions, and not just the research staff.

Another way to improve investment compensation is to introduce performance-based fees. Our strong preference is for high water marking fees and performance. In other words, the manager that relatively beats the benchmark, but still loses money for the client does not, in our opinion, deserve outsized compensation. There is a theory that active managers perform better during periods of overall market decline. One way to leverage that is to alter the fee structure to encourage neutral to positive returns in down market periods. If a manager cannot deliver better than a benchmark – say, a highly-rated sovereign credit's return over a similar time horizon – then they shouldn't be paid for their performance.

Chapter review

ROAM's final chapter focused on the firm-level structure and decisions that need to be put in place to ensure harmony with the investment management strategy. Absent this harmony, frictions are sure to bleed alpha out of investment returns.

Key considerations are: managing individual funds, first, and the firm, second; ensuring that the research staff is considered a client of each of a firm's departments; improving research staff hiring practices; looking for research staff candidates who are curious systems thinkers; and promoting and compensating staff to deliver performance in accord with the investment strategy.

Conclusion

Active equity faces a burning bridge as money pours into low-cost passive competitors. A major reason for these flows is an MPT-supported closet indexing factory within the industry that incents active funds to turn themselves into underperformers. Investors have wised up to this gambit and our heading for the exits.

In a parallel and related evolution, the industry is moving away from discredited MPT and towards behavioral finance. These two transitions challenge the current active equity ecosystem used for evaluating and selecting funds, but, on the other hand, present new opportunities for active equity investment teams.

We wrote *Return of the Active Manager* (*ROAM*) primarily for those equity teams who currently are or wish to become truly active and strive to generate alpha for their investors, while avoiding the temptation to turn themselves into closet indexers. We provide prescriptions for how this can be accomplished.

Our bottom line is that truly active equity managers, in seeking alpha, must be permitted to consistently pursue a narrowly-defined investment strategy. In other words, investors and the industry must allow them to *roam* about the equity universe in pursuit of best idea stocks.

Viewing markets as they are

Our starting point is viewing markets as they are, rather than as others would like them to be. We identify four behavioral financial market concepts:

1. Market prices are mainly driven by emotional crowds.

2. Investors are not rational, financial markets are not informationally efficient.

3. There are hundreds of behavioral price distortions (anomalies) that investors can exploit.

4. Managing emotions is the most important determinant of long-horizon wealth.

While it may seem a step backward to view markets through the lens of behavior, it turns out it provides a more reliable foundation for making investment decisions. The reason is that individuals rarely change their behavior, particularly as part of a crowd.

Behavioral wealth advisors

We begin with the critical behavioral coaching role played by financial advisors in helping clients avoid emotional decisions that can significantly reduce long-horizon wealth. Importantly, the advisor needs to encourage a long-term view of portfolio decisions by not responding to short-term volatility, drawdown, and tracking error.

The most successful advisors we refer to as *behavioral wealth advisors*, as they focus on providing a reassuring behavioral client experience while outsourcing other activities, including investment management. Such advisors grow faster and end up with a wealthy and loyal clientele.

Behaviorally-enhanced investment process

For a full ROAM to take place, investment pros must become masters of their own behaviors. Specifically, three key points in the investment process are crucial to improving returns: less biased information and data filtering; more comprehensive measurement of opinions and conclusions about information and data; and gaining greater focus and awareness about our thinking, such as that afforded by a meditation practice, or utilizing artificial means to do the same, such as leading-edge software.

Behaviorally-enhanced fundamental analysis

Embedded in financial statements and all of the various corporate communications from a business, including annual reports, press releases, conference presentations, and so on, are evidence of the actions, behaviors, choices, decisions, and ethics (ABCDE) of its people. Because personal habits are hard to change, even for seasoned executives, and a company's culture even more difficult, an analysis of this behavioral evidence can lead to unique and key insights. In brief, it is the mirrored twin of the quant stuff you do already when conducting fundamental analysis.

Let them ROAM

The key to generating superior returns is to focus on an investment team's best idea stocks. Anything that gets in the way of this pursuit hurts returns. When funds are asked to manage short-term volatility and drawdown or avoid tracking error, it hurts performance. When a fund is asked to remain in an externally imposed style box which has little to do with the fund's investment strategy, it hurts performance. When a fund is asked to closely track an index, it hurts performance, since you cannot beat an index by looking like the index.

These constraints are imposed by what we call the closet indexing factory. Using the MPT measures of volatile, beta, correlation, Sharpe ratio, information ratio, tracking error, and others, factory analysts throttle the stock picking skill of active managers. In many cases, the fund distribution system has become so beholden to these measures that only closet indexers can make it through the screening process: closet indexers need only apply!

Instead, this ecosystem needs to be refocused on manager behavior. Managers who consistently pursue a narrowly-defined strategy while focusing on high-conviction stocks outperform. Manager behavior is predictive of future fund performance where past performance is not.

Put simply, let managers *roam* the equity universe in pursuit of best ideas.

Harnessing big data

Big data is used everywhere in the investment management industry. It is increasingly used for managing equity portfolios. The challenge when building investment strategies based on big data is very noisy return data and the bane of data snooping.

Potential strategy ideas come from multiple sources, including trade and academic articles, discussions with other professionals, conferences, and so on. After being tested on as large a time series and cross-sectional data set as possible, the best outcome is a benchmark-beating return that is both statistically and economically significant. The latter is the most important as there are situations in which economically significant but statistically insignificant ideas should still be turned into an investment offering.

Once implemented, the concern is, that as others begin pursing the same strategy, the opportunity is arbitraged away. There is many a limit to arbitrage (LTA) standing in the way of full elimination. The best strategy is one that is defended by a wide LTA moat that is expected to last into the foreseeable future. Key to successful implementation is that the manager cannot respond to LTAs as others do, thus maintaining a contrary view when making investment decisions.

Importance of investment firm structure

Last among ROAM's insights is for investment firms to begin to architect better firm structures to minimize bias, and most importantly, to let their highly skilled pros *roam*!

We have addressed the full gambit from behavioral financial markets, to financial advising, to behaviorally-enhanced fundamental analysis, to active equity fund evaluation and selection, to harnessing big data to investment firm structure. In each case we provided specific prescriptions for how to create an ecosystem that favors alpha-generating active equity management.

The resulting transition will not be easy and will take time. But the result will be superior investment performance for our end clients.

Now let's get out there and ROAM!